"In *What Really Matters*, Hal addresses a challenge we all face—how to make a difference without burning out and sacrificing relationships. The principles in this book are both valuable and applicable, regardless of whether you're leading a global ministry or a group of friends."

Craig Groeschel, pastor of Life.Church and
New York Times bestselling author

"Hal's work with Convoy of Hope, which helps millions of people in need worldwide, is a beautiful story in its own right. However, this is more than that—this is a story that will cause you to imagine how God can use the difficulty you have faced for his glory."

Jennie Allen, *New York Times* bestselling author
of *Find Your People* and *Get Out of Your Head*
and founder and visionary of IF:Gathering

"Hal Donaldson has given his life to making a difference in this world and helping those in great need. He has led this charge with utmost integrity. In *What Really Matters*, Hal gives an honest and vulnerable view of not only the reward but the cost of daring greatly. I highly recommend this book to any hopeful world changer!"

Chris Tomlin, Grammy Award–winning musician and songwriter

"Vulnerability, authenticity, and transparency, undergirded with the finished work of Jesus Christ, change the world. My dear friend Hal Donaldson delivers a life-changing message adhering to the aforementioned rubric. This book is much more than a must-read. This is a must-do!"

Samuel Rodriguez, lead pastor of New Season, president/CEO of NHCLC, author of *You Are Next* and *Your Mess, God's Miracle*, and executive producer of *Breakthrough* and *Flamin' Hot*

"*What Really Matters* reminds us that servant leadership begins with stewarding our own health and well-being. As president and founder of the faith-based nonprofit Convoy of Hope, Hal Donaldson knows firsthand that self-care is not a luxury but a necessity in order to fulfill God's calling in our lives. Hal reveals how overcoming fatigue, distractions, and burnout only happens when we trust God enough to rest in him more than our own efforts. Every leader needs this book!"

Chris Hodges, senior pastor of Church of the Highlands
and author of *Out of the Cave* and *Pray First*

"We believe wholeheartedly in everything Hal Donaldson and Convoy of Hope stand for. And we are thankful for all they do to help make this world a better place. They are an organization worthy of standing with."

Ben and **Ashley Roethlisberger,** all-pro quarterback, Pittsburg Steelers; Roethlisberger Family Foundation

"*What Really Matters* is a deep exhale and look back at the greatness accomplished by a family who puts the needs of others first. There is an honest recognition of the cost of selfless living and a question put forward for us as we turn each page: Is it possible to love my spouse [and children] well while caring for the poor, the widow, and the orphan? We wrestle with this question alongside our friends and mentors, Hal and Doree Donaldson, and are grateful that the conversation is being widened."

Mōriah and **Joel Smallbone,** artist and actress; for KING & COUNTRY

"*What Really Matters* is a captivating and poignant exploration of the profound impact made by Convoy of Hope, a true beacon of altruism and resilience in a world often filled with despair. This testament to the power of collective goodwill is a must-read for anyone seeking to navigate life with greater compassion and understanding . . . more relevant today than ever before."

Kathy Ireland, actress, entrepreneur, and philanthropist

"I highly recommend *What Really Matters* from my friend and world-class leader, Hal Donaldson. Loaded with divine insight and compelling stories, this book will infuse you to change your world."

Mariano Rivera, Hall of Fame pitcher for the New York Yankees

WHAT
REALLY
MATTERS

WHAT REALLY MATTERS

HOW TO CARE FOR YOURSELF *AND* SERVE A HURTING WORLD

HAL DONALDSON
WITH LINDSAY DONALDSON-KRING

BakerBooks

a division of Baker Publishing Group
Grand Rapids, Michigan

Published by Baker Books
a division of Baker Publishing Group
Grand Rapids, Michigan
BakerBooks.com

Printed in the United States of America

Library of Congress Cataloging-in-Publication Data
Names: Donaldson, Hal, author. | Donaldson-Kring, Lindsay, author.
Title: What really matters : how to care for yourself and serve a hurting world / Hal
    Donaldson with Lindsay Donaldson-Kring.
Description: Grand Rapids, Michigan : Baker Books, a division of Baker Publishing
    Group, [2024] | Includes bibliographical references.
Identifiers: LCCN 2023043108 | ISBN 9781540903716 (cloth) | ISBN 9781493444151
    (ebook)
Subjects: LCSH: Health—Religious aspects—Christianity. | Well-being—Religious
    aspects—Christianity. | Self-care, Health.
Classification: LCC BT732 .D655 2024 | DDC 261.8/321—dc23/eng/20231201
LC record available at https://lccn.loc.gov/2023043108

Unless otherwise indicated, Scripture quotations are from the Holy Bible, New International Version®, NIV®. Copyright © 1973, 1978, 1984, 2011 by Biblica, Inc.® Used by permission of Zondervan. All rights reserved worldwide. www.zondervan.com. The "NIV" and "New International Version" are trademarks registered in the United States Patent and Trademark Office by Biblica, Inc.®

Scripture quotations labeled AMP are from the Amplified Bible. Copyright © 1954, 1958, 1962, 1964, 1965, 1987 by The Lockman Foundation. Used by permission.

Scripture quotations labeled ESV are from The Holy Bible, English Standard Version® (ESV®). Copyright © 2001 by Crossway, a publishing ministry of Good News Publishers. Used by permission. All rights reserved. ESV Text Edition: 2016

Scripture quotations labeled MSG are from *The Message*. Copyright © 1993, 2002, 2018 by Eugene H. Peterson. Used by permission of NavPress. All rights reserved. Represented by Tyndale House Publishers.

Scripture quotations labeled NET are from the NET Bible®. Copyright © 1996, 2019 by Biblical Studies Press, L.L.C. http://netbible.com. Used by permission. All rights reserved.

Scripture quotations labeled NLT are from the *Holy Bible*, New Living Translation. Copyright © 1996, 2004, 2015 by Tyndale House Foundation. Used by permission of Tyndale House Publishers, Carol Stream, Illinois 60188. All rights reserved.

Scripture quotations labeled TPT are from The Passion Translation®. Copyright © 2017, 2018, 2020 by Passion & Fire Ministries, Inc. Used by permission. All rights reserved. ThePassionTranslation.com.

Jacket design by Laura Powell

Some names and details have been changed to protect the privacy of the individuals involved.

The authors are represented by the Christopher Ferebee Agency, www.christopherferebee.com.

Baker Publishing Group publications use paper produced from sustainable forestry practices and postconsumer waste whenever possible.

24 25 26 27 28 29 30   7 6 5 4 3 2 1

Dedicated to my mother and grandmother,
who taught me the power of persistence.

CONTENTS

FOREWORD

A few years ago, one of my professors in the DMin program at Denver Seminary, Dr. Brad Strait, effectively nailed me to my chair with this simple observation: "Jesus's earthly ministry happened at the pace of approximately three miles per hour because he walked everywhere he went." In all my years of study and poring over the Bible, I'd never once thought about the pace of our Messiah's praxis. How he never missed a "God moment"—well, because he is God!— but besides that massive theological given, Jesus did life in the unforced rhythm of grace. He lived unhurriedly enough to be extraordinarily interruptible. Lepers were able to ask him for help when he and the disciples ambled past on their way to town. He sat still long enough for children to climb into his lap for a story and a cuddle. He looked deep into lonely people's eyes because he wasn't staring at his phone.

I can't help but wonder how many miracles I've hurried past on any given day to finish my to-do list. Frankly, I've spent way too much of my adult life working as if my worth depended on it—as if all the midnight oil I was burning for "kingdom purposes" was adding up in some sort of divine frequent flyer program.

When Hal and Doree graciously invited me to pen the foreword for this wonderful book, I thought they were teasing because self-care is not my strong suit! But I'm very grateful they overlooked that inauspicious detail and allowed me to peruse an advance copy of *What Really Matters*, because it's been both a template and a testimony to help me adapt my rhythm to a more sustainable and God-honoring pace. Plus, it's written with such empathy and authenticity that I didn't have to choke down guilt to get the message!

In *What Really Matters*, Hal (whom I deeply respect, so it's a bit awkward for me to address him by his first name without adding a "Mister"!) shares readily applicable principles of Christ-centered self-care against the backdrop of his story and the story of Convoy of Hope, an international faith-based nonprofit that helps millions around the world. But please know this book isn't a PR piece that touts an impressive personal résumé or global ministry efficacy. Instead, it's encouraging and relatable because it's about one man's genuine journey with Jesus to try to help the poor and powerless, the missed and marginalized, while not damaging himself or his relationships in the process.

Christ-centered self-care has been discussed a lot in faith communities over the last several years, but often only in the context of specific groups like single parents or those who have recently gone through a divorce or lost a loved one. However, self-care isn't "just" for image bearers in crisis or limited to those seasons when we feel like we can't carry the weight of our own lives anymore. Instead, it's for all of us, all the time. Furthermore, contrary to what's often modeled and applauded in communities of faith, caring for ourselves is not selfish.

In fact, God modeled self-care when he crashed out on a celestial couch after breathing the world into existence (Gen. 2:2–3). Plus, he rested before the fall, so self-care isn't an accommodation for human weakness or sin—it's our Creator Redeemer's merciful provision for our protection because he loves us unconditionally and is absolutely for us! Please consider this lovely book and the life-giving hope on every page as a gift from your heavenly Father, chosen especially for you. Then take a few deep breaths before turning the page and remember the promise Jesus proclaims to those of us whose hearts have been worn thin:

> Come to me, all you who are weary and burdened, and I will give you rest. Take my yoke upon you and learn from me, for I am gentle and humble in heart, and you will find rest for your souls. For my yoke is easy and my burden is light. (Matt. 11:28–30)

Warmest regards,
Lisa Harper

INTRODUCTION

It should have been one of the most fulfilling days of my life. Instead, my joy was threatened by an avalanche of harsh memories and pent-up emotion. More than one thousand guests had gathered to celebrate the grand opening of Convoy of Hope's new distribution center. Two governors presented inspiring speeches, business and church leaders offered meaningful testimonials, and a series of compelling videos played. Despite the enthusiastic crowd and festivities, I felt more like an embattled survivor than a CEO. Other than my wife and four daughters, few knew the toll it had taken on me to launch and steward one of the nation's fifty largest charities.

That day, I should have been celebrating the two hundred million people Convoy of Hope had served and the $2 billion in food and supplies distributed. Instead—alone in my thoughts—I reflected on the hard times: the loneliness, personal attacks, scarcity of resources, misunderstandings, nights away from my family, and lost loved ones. As applause echoed throughout the cavernous distribution center and the audience stood to its feet, I held back tears of joy mingled with regret. My wife and daughters were seated on the front row, and I couldn't help but ponder the price *they* had paid.

In my quest to feed hungry children around the world, serve disaster survivors, and help impoverished families, how many band concerts and soccer games had I missed? When my daughter Erin-Rae broke her arm, I was in a remote village in northern Kenya, delivering water to drought-stricken families. When my daughter Lauren scored her first goal, I was in New Orleans responding to Hurricane Katrina. They had every reason to be resentful and rebellious. Even my wife, Doree, could have checked out. After all, many days she was filling the shoes of mother and father. I didn't doubt my family's love for me or their admiration for the work of Convoy of Hope, but had they ever questioned how much I cherished them? They must have felt neglected and, at times, even abandoned. When I was home, I worked hard to make up for lost time. I planned special vacations, took my daughters on "daddy dates," told nightly bedtime stories, and hugged them tightly every chance I could. But there's only so much you can do when you're away from home 150 nights a year. I knew I had stretched Doree's limits, my limits—and perhaps God's too.

As the grand opening ceremony for the distribution center came to a close, we also broke ground for a new global headquarters and state-of-the-art training center. I had a shovel in my hand when I was summoned backstage to meet with Betty Cribbs. The distribution center had been named after Betty and her late husband, David. They had purchased Convoy of Hope's first tractor-trailer and played a significant role in acquiring 230 acres for the new campus in Springfield, Missouri. During some of our most trying days, David and Betty prayed and offered loads of encouragement. And when our car was pushing 150,000 miles, David and Betty gave us their new BMW. That act of generosity came at a time when we needed to know God was with us. We knew they walked close to God and listened to his voice.

"Betty," I said, "I only wish David was here with us today."

She replied, "I know he's looking down from heaven."

"Yes, I believe that," I said with a smile.

"Hal, there's something I need to tell you," she said, motioning for me to come closer. The center was still buzzing, so I turned my ear toward Betty and leaned in so I could hear every word.

"God wants you to trust him for more," she whispered. "There is much more he wants to do here. You've trusted him for thousands and millions of dollars. Now, he wants you to believe him for tens of millions. This is just the beginning."

At that moment, the floodgates opened. Tears gushed down my cheeks. Through Betty, God delivered a timely message. I could almost hear him saying, *Hal, I understand where you're at. I know better than anyone the challenges you've faced. But you can stop staring in the rearview mirror. Fix your eyes on the task ahead. There are millions who still need help now and hope for eternity. Yes, at times you've been mistreated and misunderstood, but you don't need to look over your shoulder. The past is the past. I have blessed you—and protected you and your family. I am with you.*

That afternoon, on the drive home from the grand opening, Jesus and I had a celebration. At the top of my lungs,

I said, "Thank you, Jesus. Thank you for all you've done." My shirtfront was drenched with tears of gratitude. My smile felt like it was touching my ears. I glanced at the speedometer and noticed that, without realizing it, I was driving 92 in a 65 mph zone. I pumped the brakes, but my heart was so full of joy I could have walked home. Through all the disappointments and hardships, Jesus still had me in his sights. He was never distracted or disinterested. The enemy of this world wanted me to look back and be crippled by the arduous journey. God wanted me to process the past and focus on the opportunities and miracles just around the corner.

Holy Pep Talks

Everyone needs pep talks. The Bible is filled with examples of people at the end of their rope. Elijah, for example, was so discouraged he wanted to die. "'I have had enough, LORD,' he said. 'Take my life; I am no better than my ancestors'" (1 Kings 19:4). On occasion, we all need to be reminded this isn't the end. There is hope. We need a pat on the back that urges us to press on—to persevere in the face of opposition and hardship. No one likes pain and suffering. Nor do we enjoy conflict. But sometimes it's difficult to persevere because we haven't learned how to care for ourselves.

I hope my story and the lessons I've learned will be a guidebook of sorts for taking care of *yourself* and staying encouraged while you endeavor to serve a hurting world.

God is for you. But perhaps, because of adverse circumstances or a myriad of factors, you have doubted *his* care and concern. You've questioned whether he even knows what you're going through. That's understandable, especially when your world seems to be caving in and you feel alone. You don't need to feel guilty or ashamed for those emotions. Regardless of where you are today, God wants to assure you of his love and attention. He is with you, and he's at work on your behalf. Like he told Joshua, he's saying to you, "Be strong and courageous. Do not be afraid; do not be discouraged, for the LORD your God will be with you wherever you go" (Josh. 1:9).

I'm learning that caring for my mental, spiritual, and physical health is a partnership between God and me. He will do his part. But I also need to do mine. Sometimes we wallow in pain because we don't take advantage of the tools God has given us to care for ourselves. Other times we suffer because we make sacrifices he didn't ask us to make. This book will help you do your part to care for yourself, with a full understanding that we all need God's provision and influence in every aspect of our lives.

Yes, the world is broken and in crisis, but Jesus isn't conceding anything. He wants to partner with you to distribute lasting hope to people in need. You weren't created to be a victim. You're an overcomer who has been raised up by almighty God to bring hope and healing to the world. But if you don't take care of yourself and guard your heart, you are accepting less than what God intends and promises. He doesn't ask you to serve others from a constant deficit. Have you ever tried to help others when you're running on empty and lacking stamina? God wants you to serve others from a place of wholeness.

God is infinitely powerful; people are not. Your physical, emotional, and spiritual health affect the well-being of those

Jesus has called you to serve. In this way, doing your part to care for yourself is not an act of selfishness—it is a necessary component of selflessness.

Self-care can help us "build resilience, cope with difficult life events and improve relationships."[1] But in the past, I largely viewed self-care as optional. Breaking away from a hectic schedule to recharge was a luxury reserved for planned vacations with my wife and daughters. That approach didn't serve me well, and it took me years to realize it. "If we don't practice self-care," says Dr. Sam Zand, a clinical psychiatrist, "we store unhealthy patterns in our neural pathways."[2]

> Doing your part to care for yourself is not an act of selfishness—it is a necessary component of selflessness.

Renewing Your Mind

The good news is we can change the structure of our neural pathways through what is called neuroplasticity.[3] In short, this describes how our brains change in response to the objects of our attention. "So, when Scriptures tell us to *think on what is true, honorable, pure, lovely, and good, to think on what is excellent and worthy of praise* in Philippians 4:8, this is not just a platitude to 'think happy thoughts,'" says Dr. Erin I. Smith, a professor of psychology at California Baptist University. "I think that Paul is pointing us to focus on these things because what we pay attention to changes us."[4] Learning about this, I was reminded of Romans 12:2: "Be transformed by the renewing of your mind." God designed

20

us with the ability to change, grow, and become more like Jesus.

Regardless of the challenges you face, rest assured Jesus knows how you feel. In the Gospels, we see he experienced persecution, loneliness, betrayal, conflict, weariness, a demanding schedule, and more. But time and again, he broke away from the crowds and obligations to pray, get refreshed, and gain perspective.

This book was written to help you prioritize your health and discover ways to remain encouraged. If, at times, you feel the world is against you and the target on your back is the size of a billboard, this book is for you. If you're a leader who is traversing land mines and navigating explosive personalities, this book is for you. If you're new to Jesus and still figuring out what part he plays in your life, this book is for you. Or if you're retired and have served Jesus for fifty years, this book will provide you with valuable tools.

Regardless of our starting point, God is anxious to meet us wherever we are. He's never agitated by our detours and derailments. He simply takes us by the hand, ministers to our needs, and says, *It's time to go—there are hurting people who need our help.*

Why Scars Remain

When I was twelve years old, God saw my need and came to my rescue. On the way to a business meeting, my parents were hit by a drunk driver. My father was killed instantly, and my mother suffered numerous broken bones and internal injuries. The shards of glass from the shattered windshield left her face scabbed and scarred. When I was finally allowed to see her in the hospital, I fainted. I couldn't believe I was looking at my mother.

Because my parents and the other driver didn't have insurance, and my mother was unable to work for some time, our family survived on welfare and food stamps. My three younger siblings and I experienced the pain and shame of poverty. I lived with a piercing sense of inferiority and embarrassment. Because I belonged to a lower socioeconomic class, I found it hard to look people in the eye. I was more inclined to bow to the upper class than shake their hands.

"Independence is a core value in Western culture," according to an article in the *International Journal of Environmental Research and Public Health*. "People who need help to meet a basic need, such as food, are viewed as dependent and dependency is humiliating."[5] (This is why Convoy of Hope makes it a priority to bolster the dignity of those we serve.)

I learned firsthand how poverty can erode self-worth. Some days we were forced to go to school without a lunch because the cupboards were empty. And on occasion, we had holes in our shoes and holes in our jeans (and this was before it was cool to have holey jeans.) When we couldn't afford real haircuts, we trimmed our hair ourselves. In fact, we looked punk before there was such a thing.

Despite those experiences, I wasn't overcome with bitterness at God because I also witnessed the power of kindness. Members of a local church brought groceries to our door, refurbished our home, and even put new shoes on our feet. One Sunday, a woman at church noticed I had holes in my sneakers and asked permission to take me to Kinney's shoe store. Back then, Kinney's offered three pairs of sneakers: one for $2.99, another for $3.99, and the nicest pair for $4.99.

(Times have certainly changed.) When I walked into Kinney's, I naturally made a beeline to the shoes costing $2.99. That's all I had ever known. But that day, the woman waved me over to the shoes for $4.99. She said, "Hal, today, Jesus wants you to have the best they have."

Even with such incredible kindness, my mother fought to cope with her new reality. She worked long hours to put food on the table, despite being paid far less than her male colleagues. The damage to her hip and ankle, which had been pinned back together after the accident, left her with a noticeable limp. And she was now raising four small children alone. But my mom refused to quit. She was strong—and so was her prayer life.

Some nights I would hunker down outside her bedroom door and listen to her cry and pray herself to sleep. Her circumstances seemed so unfair and unjust. I couldn't understand how a loving God could allow my father to be taken from us, while the man who hit them walked out of jail forty-eight hours later. Meanwhile, our family was sentenced to a life of poverty.

A myriad of questions raged inside me. I asked, "God, where are you? Don't you see what we're going through? Did you cause my dad to die? Did you allow him to die for a reason? Or did it just happen by chance?" Those unresolved questions haunted me for years and caused me to question God's care for me and his sovereignty in my life.

Then, as a student at San Jose State University, I wandered into a church service one Sunday night. The pastor preached a message on God's plan and destiny for our lives, based on Jeremiah 29:11: "'For I know the plans I have for you,' declares the LORD, 'plans to prosper you and not to harm you, plans to give you hope and a future.'" That night, God reassured me he was still behind the control panel of the universe, and he had a plan for my life. I hated losing my father—and I didn't have many answers—but I concluded God was good and I either had to trust him or bail out on faith altogether. Either he was real or I was on my own. There was no neutral space; I either had to follow Jesus or brand him a fraud. Ultimately, the thought of living without him and his help was too frightening. A universe absent of God didn't add up for me.

I decided to go all-in. And, years later, God would take the tragedy in my life and use it to spark the work of Convoy of Hope. But that miracle began when I placed my fate and my future in his hands.

Every Step Counts

I wish I could say all my questions vanished when I confirmed my faith in Jesus. If anything, it only summoned more questions. I also wish I could say all the trauma of my childhood was completely healed. The truth is I still have scars. But my questions, wounds, and unpleasant memories are no longer holding me back. They no longer pose threats or create obstacles because God and I have an understanding: I'm going to take care of myself—and endeavor to become more like Jesus—and entrust my past and future to him. That is the promise of 1 Peter 5:7: "Cast all your anxiety on him because he cares for you."

You may have unresolved issues or deep disappointments that are preventing you from walking into the plans God has for you. Maybe you've suffered from a divorce, health crisis, or financial setback. Regardless, it is not his desire for you to be haunted by unpleasant memories. You do not have to be trapped by the pain of your past any longer. As you read *What Really Matters*, ask God to fill your soul with hope and vitality. Invite him to reveal his path to wholeness and forgiveness. He wants to take this journey with you, because the course is not clearly marked point A to point B. At times you may trip and fall. But you can count on God to be there to pick you up, dust you off, and offer words of encouragement.

As an adult, when my heart was aching with disappointment, I sank into periods of discouragement. The actions of others left me metaphorically bleeding out on the side of the road. Thankfully, I found healing and peace when I realized God the Father and his Son, Jesus, knew how I felt. God was betrayed by Satan, and Jesus was betrayed by Judas. They knew my struggle. So, whenever indignation and grief reared their ugly heads, I could find comfort and perspective by going to a "fellow sufferer" in prayer.

Breaking free from the grasp of one's past—and the grip of one's enemy—is not as simple as "ten easy steps." You can think of this book as less self-help (which often focuses on an event) and more self-care (which is a lifestyle). There are actions you can take to improve your quality of life and draw closer to Jesus, but the road to wholeness begins with adjusting your expectations. Remember, you are embarking on an uncharted adventure to an unknown destination. En route, you can anticipate new discoveries and occasional disappointments. Some days won't feel perfect, but with each step you're closer to the life God has promised. Songwriter Steffany Gretzinger puts this in perspective in her song "Oxygen": "Baby steps and short breaths / anything is progress."[6]

You can begin to breathe again with this simple prayer: "Jesus, you know me better than I know myself. Help me understand what really matters to you. And help me discover ways to move beyond my pain and embrace the new beginning you have for me."

1

DEADLY EXPECTATIONS

But a huge crowd from Galilee trailed after them—also from
Judea, Jerusalem, Idumea, across the Jordan, and around
Tyre and Sidon—swarms of people who had heard the reports and had come to see for themselves. He told his disciples to get a boat ready so he wouldn't be trampled by the
crowd. He had healed many people, and now everyone who
had something wrong was pushing and shoving to get near
and touch him.

Mark 3:7–10 MSG

The sun was especially bright for a November day in Missouri. Its rays were glinting off my computer screen, so
I vaulted from my seat at my desk to adjust the blinds. Immediately I felt a sharp pain below my shoulder blades, and
I fell back into my chair. Years earlier, I had passed a kidney
stone, and this felt similar, so I self-diagnosed that another

"boulder" was attempting to enter my urinary canal. I drove myself home, dropped two Tylenol, and awaited my wife's return.

An hour passed, with the pain increasing in intensity, and finally Doree was home.

"Doree," I said. "I think you'd better drive me to Emergency. They'll give me some medicine to help pass the stone."

Forty-five minutes later, I was sitting in a wheelchair with a blood pressure sleeve attached to my arm. When the nurse's face blanched, I knew this was more serious than a kidney stone.

"What's happening?" I asked.

"I don't think this is a kidney stone—it could be your heart," she replied.

Seconds later, I was being hoisted onto a gurney and rushed down the hallway into surgery by an entourage of medical professionals. Even though death appeared to be knocking at my door and my blood pressure was skyrocketing, it was the calmest moment of my life. While doctors and nurses scurried to their stations, I whispered a prayer. No panic. Just peace.

"God, if this is the end of my journey, thank you for giving me a great life. I've been blessed. All I ask is that you take care of Doree and the girls." Those were my final words before the anesthesia kicked in and the physician commenced with the angiogram.

When I awoke the next morning, Doree and my friend Mart Green were standing at the end of my bed. Mart had driven through the night to be by my side and pray for me.

"Am I going to be okay?" I asked, seeking confirmation.

"Yes, everything's good now," Doree said, leaning over the bed for a kiss.

"You're going to be better than okay, my man," Mart added, taking hold of my hand. "God has more for you to do."

Tears welled up in my eyes because, at that moment, I knew God was giving me another chance.

Doree delivered the prognosis: "The doctor will be here shortly, but they had to put two stents in your left artery. But they said the rest of the heart looked fine, and you'll be okay."

In the days that followed, as I lay in my hospital bed, I prayed for understanding and direction. I opened my Bible at random one night and began reading Psalm 138. My eyes fell on these words: "Though I walk in the midst of trouble, you preserve my life" (Ps. 138:7).

God hadn't called me to be a martyr, but I'd been living like one. I was working two jobs, speaking on weekends, and authoring books. It was obvious the demanding schedule and prolonged stress had contributed to my illness. It was time to make some serious changes, or there would be more stents in my future. I'm certain God tried to get my attention long before—I just wasn't listening. But now I was hearing him loud and clear. If I didn't make changes and learn to deal with my stress, my stress was going to deal with me. In my attempt to live up to other people's expectations and ac- complish more for God, I had maintained an unhealthy pace. Burnout is the result of misplaced priorities—either you're running too fast or resting too little. I checked both boxes.

Shortly after being released from the hospital, I resigned my position as editor-in-chief of a magazine, canceled two book contracts, cleared my speaking calendar, and stepped off the boards of several ministries. It was time to focus on my health and family and devote my full attention to the mission of Convoy of Hope.

Regrettably, my pledge to make such life changes was short-lived. As my physical strength rebounded, so did my sense of obligation. Within months, I found myself traveling extensively and responding to new ministry opportunities. Meanwhile, for Doree and our daughters, it was like watching a bad television rerun. I resumed working sixty-hour weeks, responding to nightly phone calls, and filling my calendar with appointments. In addition, I was giving the girls front-row seats to the perils of leadership. My youngest daughter, Haly, said it best: "Sometimes leadership just isn't fun, because people try to place unrealistic expectations on you." She nailed it—but most of the blame rested on my shoulders. I failed to respond appropriately to others' expectations, which manifested in undue stress.

Of course, some pressure is necessary and beneficial. It can help motivate us to accomplish God's will. But an inner voice that incessantly demands we do more and more is not from God. In our quest to please him, he never asks us to sacrifice ourselves and others. Someday, we *don't* want Jesus to hand us the deed to what we built and hear him say, "This belongs to you—I had nothing to do with it."

Great Expectations

Years earlier, I was honored to be appointed editor-in-chief of the magazine of the Assemblies of God fellowship. Based in Springfield, Missouri, the denomination had grown to eighty-five million members worldwide. At one time, my grandfather served as one of the national leaders in the church. He was a gifted speaker, accomplished administrator, and visionary. His future appeared bright. But then it was discovered he was having an extramarital affair with a coworker. He was subsequently relieved from his position. Humiliated and ashamed, he packed up his family and belongings and drove away from Springfield, never to return. In the years that followed, he divorced my grandmother and suffered a stroke that paralyzed one side of his body. He passed away before I had a chance to really know him.

On my last day in California before moving to Missouri to take the editor's position, I visited my grandmother. Gram possessed the elegance of a 1940s movie star, always wearing lipstick and "zhuzhing" her hair. Despite suffering her husband's betrayal, she had maintained a kind and generous heart. I admired her resilience and respected her faith. Following my father's death, she lived with our family and assisted my mother for many months. Although she worked part-time in a clothing store, she assumed much of the cooking and laundry duties and, each morning, made sure we boarded the school bus on time.

"Honey," she said, "I believe God is sending you to Springfield for more than a job. I think he's taking you there to restore our family name. God is giving us another chance. Your grandfather became proud and ambitious, and it cost him everything. He couldn't handle the power or the stress. Don't go there trying to make things happen for yourself. Let God do it. Guard your heart and stay humble. If you do that, you'll be surprised by what he does through you."

With tears in our eyes, we embraced. "I'm proud of you," she said. "I'll pray for you every day."

That conversation would influence my actions and decisions for the next two decades. When I arrived in Springfield, honoring my mother and grandmother and restoring our family name became a primary objective. Gram never intended to place heavy expectations on me. But from the outset, I wanted to make her dream come true. After everything she'd gone through, she deserved a happy ending to the story.

Ask yourself, *Am I living under the pressure of someone's expectations? Perhaps a parent or sibling? An employer or a child?* That can prove to be a major source of stress, especially when those expectations are unreasonable. The fear of disappointing others can lead to poor decisions, such as marrying the wrong person, buying a car we can't afford, accepting a job we resent, and more. However, sometimes we attribute expectations to others that are actually self-imposed. We need to be honest with ourselves about where expectations are coming from, and which ones really matter.

Disappointing God

Many live under an unspoken fear of disappointing God and not measuring up to *his* expectations. Psychologist Ed Welch of the Christian Counseling and Educational Foundation notes, "Most people I know . . . are fairly certain that God will say [to them], 'You are such a disappointment. Forgiven, but a disappointment.'"[1] To the contrary, God's expectations are realistic and woven together with grace. As you read these words from Ephesians, let each one sink in: "But because of his great love for us, God, who is rich in mercy, made us alive with Christ even when we were dead in transgressions—it is by grace you have been saved" (Eph. 2:4–5).

Jesus isn't requiring you to respond to the needs of every person who crosses your path. Nor does he expect you to become a superhero, responding to one crisis after another. He isn't scrolling others' social media threads to compile their life's highlight reels and use them as a rubric for *your* life. Yet many make the mistake of measuring their reality against the fictional lives of others.

"There are no doghouses in the Kingdom of God," Welch also says.[2] There is no punishment for shortcomings, because perfection was never God's expectation. He knows your limitations and likely expects less of you than you may think. Psalm 103:8–14 says,

> The LORD is compassionate and gracious,
>   slow to anger, abounding in love.
> He will not always accuse,
>   nor will he harbor his anger forever;
> he does not treat us as our sins deserve
>   or repay us according to our iniquities.
> For as high as the heavens are above the earth,
>   so great is his love for those who fear him;
> as far as the east is from the west,
>   so far has he removed our transgressions from us.
> As a father has compassion on his children,
>   so the LORD has compassion on those who fear
>   him;
> for he knows how we are formed,
>   he remembers that we are dust.

In my youth, I imagined God as "the great spectator in the sky" who scrutinized my every move and penalized me for each mistake. Rather than viewing him as an advocate, I saw him as a hard-to-please professor. I assumed he based my report card solely on my participation and performance, as if his favor was tied to a spreadsheet created to display my grades in real time. Every move I made had the potential to affect my standing. And every time I fell short of my God-given potential, I imagined his scorn. After all, he had every right to demand I be the perfect leader, father, husband, friend, and compassion worker. He had blessed me with so much—I assumed I was contractually obligated to reach his lofty expectations.

Some of my guilt stemmed from a misunderstanding of Scripture. In particular, I wanted to measure up to Luke 12:48: "From everyone who has been given much, much will be demanded; and from the one who has been entrusted with much, much more will be asked." If you're a Marvel fan, you may recall a similar line in Spider-Man movies: "With great power comes great responsibility."[3]

In college, I took a course on the life of Jesus and discovered that Luke 12 does not refer to personal achievement. Jesus does not demand perfection. In this chapter, he is warning against greed and hoarding resources. It's about being generous to others. For years, I'd heaped unrealistic expectations on myself that led to feelings of failure and regret.

Luke 12:15 says, "Watch out! Be on your guard against all kinds of greed; life does not consist in an abundance of possessions." And then in verse 21, we're told to avoid accumulating earthly treasures for ourselves, because that won't make us rich with God. Instead, we're instructed to store up treasures in heaven by being "open-handed" to others. And verse 34 says, "For where your treasure is, there your heart will be also." In summary, what really matters is that we have a heart after God, because that is far more valuable than money, accolades, job titles, and awards.

When I discovered Luke 12 is about serving Jesus by giving to others—*not* by being perfect—I no longer had to walk on spiritual eggshells. Throughout college, I felt liberated from the handcuffs of guilt and shame and spiritual comparisons. I began to see God for who he really is—all-powerful, all-knowing, all-loving, and abounding in mercy.

Regrettably, upon entering the workforce in my twenties, I found myself grappling with the same issues that had previously stolen my joy. Once again, I focused on performance and achievement, rather than resting in God's grace and trusting in his understanding. It would take me over thirty years to fully break free from the fear of disappointment. Apparently I wasn't a fast learner.

Making Room

Between my fear of disappointing God and my desire to fulfill others' expectations, I failed to adequately care for myself. My well-being was far down my list of priorities. In an attempt to follow Jesus and "perform Christianity" at a high level, I wasn't dealing with stress in a Christ-honoring way. Some days, I worked until two in the morning and crawled into bed long after Doree had fallen asleep. In the name of serving Jesus, I foolishly consumed caffeinated drinks to extend my work hours, compressed my personal devotions, and shortened the time I allotted for exercise.

My physical and emotional health suffered. Because I viewed my lifestyle as a necessary sacrifice for the mission, I assumed I was exempt from the consequences of an unbalanced life. Lying face up on a hospital gurney, I concluded I was very wrong.

"High levels of stress . . . [and] repeated release of the stress hormone cortisol can disturb the immune system, and raise the likelihood of developing autoimmune disorders, cardiovascular disease, and Alzheimer's disease," according to the *Harvard Health* blog.[4] We make the enemy's job easier and enlarge his target—to steal, kill, and destroy—when we consistently live with stress.

Without realizing it, I had been playing into the enemy's hands and listening to his relentless lies.

You aren't doing enough.

You're falling short of your potential and God's expectations.

You're inadequate for the task you've been given.

You've disappointed God and lost his favor.

Now you're on your own.

I had forgotten one important fact: the enemy is a liar. "The thief comes only to steal and kill and destroy; I have come that they may have life, and have it to the full" (John 10:10).

> We make the enemy's job easier and enlarge his target—to steal, kill, and destroy—when we consistently live with stress.

The enemy had deceived me into believing I was disappointing God. My drive to achieve stemmed from a fear of him rather than a deep love for him. Much of my stress was a byproduct of spiritual discontentment and a misunderstanding of God's expectations. To break free from the clutches of the enemy, I needed a revelation of what really mattered to God. I needed to know what he was asking from me.

The enemy of this world magnifies what isn't real, but your God multiplies his blessings that are real. The enemy wants you to believe God has set the bar so high you are destined to fail, and he turns speed bumps into Mount Everest. He makes puddles look like the Pacific. He wants you to fix your eyes on the obstacles, but God says, *Peer beyond the speed bumps to the blessings I have for you.* You have a choice. You can allow the lies and magnifications of the enemy to hold you back, or you can press on and place your trust in the promises of God. You can throw up your hands in frustration or turn your eyes to heaven and say, "My God is bigger than my circumstances. He is more powerful than my en-

> You can allow the lies and magnifications of the enemy to hold you back, or you can press on and place your trust in the promises of God.

emies. He understands me and, through the blood of Jesus, I have been forgiven. I refuse to allow the expectations of others or the magnifications of the enemy to dictate my future. God sees my weaknesses, my past, and my failures, and he's saying, 'I love you—I know you—let's go change the world together.'"

Your enemy wants you to live in fear of people and failure, to the point that you quit or veer off mission. His scheme is to intimidate and tempt you with dead-end promises. God wants you to live with the assurance his power will overcome the attacks of the enemy every time. The enemy's attacks are temporary, but God's power is eternal. First John 4:4 says, "You, dear children, are from God and have overcome . . . because the one who is in you is greater than the one who is in the world." In the face of uncertainty and discouragement, you are not helpless. You are not alone. The Holy Spirit is at your side.

Surveys conducted by the Barna Research Group and the
Pew Research Center reflect that Christians are more likely
to agree on their beliefs about God, Jesus, and heaven than
about Satan and hell.[5] So, for the purpose of the conversa-
tions in this book, I want to clarify what I mean when I
reference "Satan" or "the enemy."

The Bible teaches that Satan and his forces are real.
Whenever persons commit themselves to the cause of God,
evil spiritual forces will come against them. Ephesians 6:12
says, "We are not fighting against flesh-and-blood enemies,
but against evil rulers and authorities of the unseen world,
against mighty powers in this dark world, and against evil
spirits in the heavenly places" (NLT).

It is comforting to know God is in full control. Scripture
tells us he limits what evil forces can do to us. Our knowl-
edge of the spirit world, however, is limited to what God has
revealed in his Word. And from Scripture, we know Satan
isn't all-knowing, all-powerful, or present everywhere. He
can only be in one place at one time. Sometimes we assume
Satan is hiding behind every corner. But he has limits; the
God we serve doesn't.

Satan isn't the only evil actor at work. Evil can come
from many sources. Most of us will never directly encounter
Satan in a spiritual battle, but all who follow Jesus *will* be
confronted by evil spirits, people, and institutions. The great
news is we already know the ending to the story. Almighty
God has already won. And when you give your life to Jesus,
you are victorious too.

During an NBA basketball game against the Los Angeles
Lakers in 2022, one of my favorite players, Stephen Curry,
had a game to remember. He drained threes from every

angle, made dazzling passes, and scored on driving layups. His opponent was a consummate trash-talker, but even he was silenced by the superstar's magnificence. After scoring another basket, Curry peered up at the crowd and yelled, "He can't stop me." The Lakers called time-out to regroup, while the Warriors coaches and players leaped to their feet in applause. Once again, their team's superstar was leading them to victory. Likewise, you can carry yourself with the same confidence and swagger because God is with you and the game has already been won. No matter what the enemy tries, he can't stop you.

2

BATTLE SCARS

Jesus came and stood among them and said, "Peace be with you!" Then he said to Thomas, "Put your finger here; see my hands. Reach out your hand and put it into my side. Stop doubting and believe."

John 20:26–27

Twelve-year-old kids shouldn't have to attend their father's funeral. But there I was, perched on the front pew with my three younger siblings, watching the nightmare unfold. Hundreds of my father's friends filed by his open casket to offer tearful goodbyes. One collapsed to the carpet as she approached, while another woman wailed in the back of the sanctuary. Many wiped their eyes with handkerchiefs as an organist played hymns in the background. Dozens watched from the foyer because every pew was filled. My father, a local pastor, was well known in the community. The morning following the accident, I'd woken to images of his face and a mangled car on the front page of the local newspaper.

At the conclusion of the viewing line, my uncle Jim whispered, "You can now go up and see your dad." I shot him a strained look. I didn't budge, because I didn't want to remember my dad as a distorted, wax-like figure in a box. Finally, Uncle Jim took my elbow and guided me to the casket. I only glanced at Dad's swollen face before closing my eyes. Tears streamed down my cheeks anyway. To myself, I said, *This isn't my father. He's in heaven. I don't want to see him like this.* I tightened my jaw. *This isn't my dad*, I repeated. I wanted the funeral to end. I didn't need any more hugs or condolences. I just wanted to be left alone with my thoughts—I had a lot to sort out. I'm sure heaven rejoiced when my father entered the pearly gates, but for me it was the saddest day of my life.

Though my face was red and tearstained, my eyes were glued to Pastor McNeven as he stepped to the pulpit to officiate the service. The night of the accident, he'd huddled the four of us kids together to pray in our front yard. He was there when we needed someone to remind us Jesus loved us and had a plan for our lives. I can't remember much of his funeral message, but his tears spoke volumes. He didn't attempt to hide his pain or questions. He said, "A few days ago, I lost my best friend . . . and one of the most Christlike men I've ever met. Honestly, I don't know why Harold Donaldson was called home to heaven, but in times like this we have to put our trust in God."

Despite Pastor McNeven's sincere directive, "trusting God" wouldn't come easy for me. I struggled to make sense of it all—none of it seemed fair or just.

The night of the accident, my siblings and I were invited to stay with Bill and Louvada Davis and their two children. We lived in their mobile home for months while my mother recovered from her injuries. One day Bill, who could see I was hurting, threw his arm over my shoulder and said, "Hal, don't allow the tragedy of your youth to become a lifelong excuse, because where you start in life doesn't have to dictate where you end." I knew Bill was right, but I needed answers before I could fully trust God again. The trauma of seeing my father's casket lowered into the ground, and the sound of my mother crying herself to sleep, left me with severe wounds. And, regrettably, emotional bandages were nowhere to be found. I had to figure things out for myself.

My experience isn't exceptional—an estimated one in thirteen (nearly 8 percent) of children in the United States will experience the death of a parent or sibling by age eighteen.[1] Everyone grieves differently, but as I researched childhood bereavement, I came across a statement that hit home:

Some people describe [the loss] as "the moment their childhood ended." . . . Children were often expected to take on more responsibility within the family. While for some this may have helped build self-reliance and empathy at an early age, for others it may also have meant their grief was not fully acknowledged or validated.[2]

The bullying I experienced in middle school only compounded my questions about justice and God. I wanted to believe he hadn't abandoned me, but many days I felt like it was me against the world. I didn't seek conflict, but at school my secondhand clothes made me an easy target. One kid spat in my face. Another hip-checked me into the lockers. Guys stole my gym clothes. To make matters worse, I felt like there was no one I could appeal to for help. I figured my mom had enough concerns—she didn't need me to add to her stack of worries. So, like many kids, I bottled up the pain and kept the struggle to myself.

When the bullies' antics became unbearable, I fought the temptation to take matters into my own hands. Fortunately, I was able to channel some of my anger onto the football field. There, I seemed to earn some respect, until I suffered a broken arm. During one game, I dropped back to throw a pass and, from behind, the rusher hit me just right. I heard my elbow snap. The remainder of the season, I was forced to cheer from the sidelines. But the news wasn't all bad: after that, none of the bullies wanted to mess with a kid wielding a bulky cast.

In high school, trash-talking on the basketball court landed me in trouble. I was having one of those days you dream about: twenty-foot jumpers, behind-the-back passes, spinning drives to the hoop. I should have let my game do the talking, but I unwisely provoked my six-four, two-hundred-pound opponent. "Todd," I taunted, "you're not good enough—let someone else try."

Afterward, Todd came looking for me in the locker room. His eyes were fireballs. "You think you're [*expletive*] cool, don't you?" I threw on my shirt and said, "I was just joking around—didn't mean anything by it."

Apparently, my answer wasn't sufficient, because he staggered me with a right hook to the jaw.

"What's your problem, man?" I exclaimed. "It's just basketball."

He clobbered me a second time.

"Todd, I get it—sorry!"

He reared back to hit me a third time, and having already turned both cheeks, I assumed I had fully complied with the teachings of Jesus. I buried my head in his chest and drove him onto his back. I'm not sure what my plan was from there, and I was exceedingly grateful that a coach intervened just in time by grabbing a wad of my shirt and lifting me off Todd.

"That's enough, you guys," he ordered. "Get dressed and get out of here." Todd lunged at me again, but the coach intercepted him. "I said go—now!" God works in mysterious ways. After news of the fight spread, no one ever bullied me again. And later, the coach congratulated me on making a "nice tackle."

Now that was satisfying.

When you are constantly put down and you compare yourself to others, you naturally feel inferior and inadequate. You become ensnared by others' opinions. Tragically, many endure abuse every day—verbally, emotionally, or physically—because of how they look, how they speak, or where they come from. It's no surprise that some choose to cope with their pain and feelings of inadequacy by burying themselves in work or turning to food, drugs, or alcohol. The scars from previous battles exist, and every day is another struggle to hide or numb the mounting pain.

There is a common expectation, particularly in Western culture, that those in pain or trouble just need to "suck it up" and "get over it" as quickly as possible. And, in many Christian faith communities, there is an even higher expectation: "Take it—smile wide and publicly display the strength of your faith." Neither of those paths is healthy or sustainable. Betsy Barber, professor at Biola's Talbot School of Theology, says,

> This is a world full of brokenness, and grief tells the truth about that brokenness. Truth is sturdy, we can build our life on truth, and truth illuminates our trajectory and gives us discernment in decisions. The truth of grief shows us the way through the experience. . . . It is human and expected and unavoidable. It is not sinful. We know this because Jesus grieved.[3]

In John 11, Jesus wept when he saw sisters Martha and Mary crying following the death of their brother Lazarus. Jesus was moved, in part, by *their* sorrow. Likewise, we have the right to grieve when hardship or death enters our orbit.

When enduring physical or emotional pain—and with no relief in sight—hope can fade into uncertainty. Following my parents' auto accident, I didn't doubt God's love. But my intense pain did cause me to question his authority. I wondered what role he played in my father's death. Was he a catalyst, bystander, or healer?

Answers from the Bible

With the guidance of my youth pastor, I found some answers in the book of Job. When catastrophe struck, Job did not allow hardship to erode his trust in the Creator. God was his healer and deliverer—not his afflicter. Job 2:7 says, "So Satan went out from the presence of the LORD and afflicted Job with painful sores from the soles of his feet to the crown of his head." Ultimately God led Job through his season erk

of pain and shame. His health was restored and his wealth multiplied. As a boy who empathized with Job, I prayed God would do the same for me.

Today I still have questions about my father's death, but I am no longer tormented by them. I've forgiven the driver who brought us so much pain, even though I don't understand how the justice system permitted him to walk away without facing consequences. I'm at peace knowing some events won't be understood on this side of heaven. Certainly pain persists and scars remain, but God doesn't waste a single broken piece from my experience or yours. We may not be able to see a completed masterpiece, but the Master is still at work on our behalf.

You may be saying, "I get it—pain isn't a waste of time! But I'm weary of the fight. I've been beaten down and tossed aside for years. I need a breakthrough. I don't want to live this way." First, never feel guilty for raw emotion. God wants an honest relationship with you, where you freely share your struggles. He's not offended by your questions or outbursts. He doesn't expect you to greet difficult and painful experiences with a smile. That's robotic. Jesus wants us to be authentic.

You may have good reason to be angry, but you do not have to park there. Jesus doesn't expect you to go through hardship alone. He is there to comfort and protect you in your time of need. The "Spirit himself intercedes for us with groanings too deep for words" (Rom. 8:26 ESV). And that doesn't apply just to trauma or painful experiences. Months, years, and decades can pass, and then something triggers your emotions and you find yourself right back where you were. Time can bring a degree of healing and perspective,

but sometimes it doesn't take much for wounds to reopen and pain to resurface. Even then, God wants you to know you can turn to him for help.

When wounds reopen, here are five promises from God's Word:

1. **Jesus understands your wounds and scars.** Isaiah 53:3 says, "He was despised and rejected by men, a man of sorrows and acquainted with grief" (ESV).

2. **God will never turn against you.** Isaiah 41:13 says, "For I am the Lord your God who takes hold of your right hand and says to you, Do not fear; I will help you."

3. **God sees your needs 24/7.** Psalm 139:7–10 says, "Where can I go from your Spirit? Where can I flee from your presence? If I go up to the heavens, you are there; if I make my bed in the depths, you are there. If I rise on the wings of the dawn, if I settle on the far side of the sea, even there your hand will guide me, your right hand will hold me fast."

4. **God hears your prayers, and he will answer.** Jeremiah 29:12–13 says, "Then you will call on me and come and pray to me, and I will listen to you. You will seek me and find me when you seek me with all your heart."

5. **Jesus is your Healer, and he sees the final outcome.** Psalm 41:3 says, "The Lord sustains them on their sickbed and restores them from their bed of illness."

Imagine that you own a treasured vase, an artifact from the age of Cleopatra that is so valuable Lloyd's of London won't present it for auction because it's considered priceless.

Unfortunately, someone knocks the vase off the mantel and it shatters into a thousand small pieces. You're afraid to touch the fragments, so you call in an expert to assist at the "crime scene." He promptly sweeps up the shards and says, "Trust me—when I'm done with it, the vase will look as good as new. On the inside there may be evidence of the injury and reconstruction, but this vase will be even stronger once I put it back together." That's what God does for you, his priceless child. He picks up the broken pieces of your life and makes you whole again. The scars are real, but now you are stronger than ever.

A Team Sport

Galatians 6:2 says, "Carry one another's burdens" (AMP). God created us with an innate need for community. He didn't intend for us to face crises and tend to our wounds alone. Yet many fail to seek his help, confide in a friend, gain biblical perspective from a pastor, or pursue guidance from a professional counselor or therapist. Are you hesitant to share the load? Is it difficult to open up to another person? Being vulnerable to the right people can be difficult, particularly if you've been betrayed

> It may appear safer to hide one's wounds and scars, but seldom is that the shortest distance to healing.

or if you're a leader under constant scrutiny. It may appear safer to hide one's wounds and scars, but seldom is that the shortest distance to healing.

The concept that life is a team sport isn't just a biblical idea—it's backed by science. "Wide-ranging research suggests that strong social ties are linked to a longer life," according to the National Institute of Health, while "Loneliness and social isolation are linked to poorer health, depression, and increased risk of early death."[4] Researchers worldwide are still gathering data on the long-term societal effects of the COVID-19 pandemic and how it enhanced feelings of isolation, fear, and loneliness; however, "Researchers realized that Americans were lonelier than ever [even] before the pandemic hit, leading them to conclude that we have an epidemic of loneliness."[5]

Making and maintaining meaningful relationships can be more challenging as an adult than when we're in high school or college, for example. I didn't have trouble making friends with guys in my dorm. We had intramural sports and loads of common interests that kept us connected. But once I entered the workforce, began raising a family, and assumed more responsibility, building substantive relationships wasn't as simple. If you're going through a season of life where relationships are harder to find, don't be discouraged. Consider whether you're placing a priority on quantity over quality, or if something such as fear of rejection could be holding you back. It's never too late to take the initiative to form deeper relationships with godly people who can help you put your scars in proper perspective.

Still Mom

After my mother was diagnosed with Alzheimer's, I began phoning her nearly every night on my way home from work. Some evenings she found it difficult to string her thoughts together, but it was always comforting to hear her voice. We had been like business partners since I was twelve, when she began asking my opinion on everything from finances to car repairs. But, even as a kid, I often worried about her. She was coping with the loss of a husband, learning to survive in a male-dominated workplace, and trying to keep four kids from going off the rails.

Some nights, when the pressure was intense, she'd drop off dinner in the kitchen and retreat to her bedroom. I knew the financial burden was relentless. She regretted having to use food stamps and was irritated each month when the social worker came to gauge our need for government assistance. "I can't wait until we're off welfare," she often said. I admired her tenacity. She had every reason to quit but never did, and she was determined to give her kids a better life.

My mother's wounds were emotional *and* physical. Her lingering hip and ankle injuries forced her to take pain medication so she could function at work. Much of her emotional scarring was kept hidden, however. Nonetheless she courageously battled through periods of depression and discouragement. There was no money for her to consult a counselor, so she pressed on without complaint. But her pain and challenges left a mark on me too.

Decades later, when my mother's physician recommended her for hospice care, we knew her battle with the disease was coming to an end. Several days before her passing, I sat in a chair next to her bed and held her hand. It was just the two of us. Her breathing was labored and her face ashen. I wasn't sure if she could hear me, but I spoke to her for over an hour anyway. There were things I needed to say.

"Mom, you are my hero," I said through tears. "I owe you my life. Thank you for not giving up. You paid a price to keep our family together, and we'll work hard at making you proud."

My mind flashed back to the first time she entered her new home in Springfield, Missouri. It was a privilege for us to hand her the keys. "You deserve this, Mom," I'd said. "This is God's way of honoring you for all you've done." Brushing tears from her face, she'd replied, "This is one of the happiest days of my life."

It was hard to believe—just a few years later—that she was on the threshold of going to heaven to be with Jesus and reunited with my dad.

"Mom," I said, still caressing her hand, "when you get to heaven, please tell Dad I miss him. And, if you have a chance, let Jesus know I could use some extra help down here. I love you with all my heart. I'm thankful to be your son."

That evening I said my farewells, realizing I might have seen her for the last time. Sitting in my car outside the nursing home, I sobbed until my voice was a whisper. Pent-up emotions emptied all at once. The disease, the disappointments, the deaths—she had endured more than her share of hardship. But now her years of struggle were coming to a close, and there was no doubt the jewels in her heavenly crown would be magnificent.

Declarations

I don't know if this description of God and his relationship with you and your scars rings true. Nor do I know if you're cautiously optimistic or find yourself doubting his promises. Regardless of where you are, Jesus will meet you there. Here are four declarations you can begin repeating to invite him into your situation:

1. **I am not fighting a losing battle.** Psalm 60:12 says, "With God we will gain the victory, and he will trample down our enemies." Victory is more than a strong possibility. Victory is guaranteed.

2. **My God is greater than my need.** Whenever I feel overwhelmed, I tell myself, *Remember Saturn.* If God can create a planet with beautiful gaseous rings, he is certainly much bigger than my troubles. Isaiah 40:11–13 says,

   > He tends his flock like a shepherd:
   >   He gathers the lambs in his arms
   > and carries them close to his heart;
   >   he gently leads those that have young.
   >
   > Who has measured the waters in the hollow of his
   >   hand,
   > or with the breadth of his hand marked off the
   >   heavens?
   > Who has held the dust of the earth in a basket,
   >   or weighed the mountains on the scales
   >   and the hills in a balance?
   > Who can fathom the Spirit of the LORD,
   >   or instruct the LORD as his counselor?

3. **I can do all things through Jesus.** Philippians 4:13 says, "Whatever I have, wherever I am, I can make it through anything in the One who makes me who I am" (MSG). The enemy wants you to focus on

what you can't do rather than on what Jesus can do through you. He wants you to emphasize your limitations, but your strength comes from the Lord. Isaiah 40:29–31 says, "He gives strength to the weary and increases the power of the weak . . . those who hope in the LORD will renew their strength. They will soar on wings like eagles; they will run and not grow weary, they will walk and not be faint."

4. **I serve a God who specializes in miracles.** Jeremiah 32:27 says, "I am the LORD, the God of all mankind. Is anything too hard for me?" If Jesus can heal lepers, restore sight to the blind, and feed thousands with a few fish and loaves of bread, he is able to meet your need too.

The memories of painful or embarrassing experiences can dwell with us for many years and influence future behavior. They can leave lasting scars. Such was the case when I spoke at a business conference in Macon, Georgia. My boss at the time was slated to speak, but when he discovered he was double-booked, he drafted me to take his place. I was only twenty-four and a novice public speaker, so I sought his advice. He said, "This is a great opportunity. It will be televised, and you'll be speaking to thousands of people. You can do this. Just make sure you're prepared—and don't blow it."

When I landed at the William B. Hartsfield Airport in Atlanta, I discovered I had forgotten my credit cards. No agency would rent me a car without a card. So I marched up to a complete stranger and said, "Sir, you don't know me and I don't know you. But I will give you $200 cash right now if you drive me to Macon, Georgia. Without hesitation, he said, "Let's go."

His car was missing hubcaps, the air conditioner was broken, and the window on the passenger side was stuck. Nevertheless, we reached my destination: the Macon Coliseum.

> **The memories of painful or embarrassing experiences can dwell with us for many years and influence future behavior. They can leave lasting scars.**

When I entered the rear door of the arena, I was met by a panicky producer wearing a headset. She said, "Mr. Donaldson, you're on in five minutes." My throat was raw and my suit terribly wrinkled, but there was no time to change clothes or collect my thoughts. Moments later, I walked onto the stage to deliver a speech to a capacity crowd. It was going well until I attempted to quote a physiologist from an article in *Time* magazine. Instead of saying physiologist, I tripped over my tongue and said, "Piss-ologist." The crowd erupted into laughter. I attempted to correct myself, and sadly, it came out the same way again. If you've never had nine thousand people laughing at you—it's humiliating. At that moment, I could have taken a stage dive into the orchestra pit. Instead, I finished my speech and walked off the stage to a smattering of applause. I never inquired if my boss heard about my blooper. All I know is he never asked me to speak for him again.

That episode left a scar on my psyche. For years after that, I over-prepared sermons and over-rehearsed speeches. I was determined to avoid embarrassing myself again. Are there unpleasant memories in your life that continue to haunt you or drive your behavior? You may never be able to look back at them with a chuckle. But, as a child of God, you can claim the promise of Psalm 91:14–15: "Because you loved me, delighted in me, and have been loyal to my name, I [the Lord] will greatly protect you. I will answer your cry for help every time you pray, and you will feel my presence in your time of trouble. I will deliver you and bring you honor" (TPT).

Today, your scars do not have to become monuments to pain. With God's help, scars can become shrines to a time he came to your rescue.

3

RECKLESS AMBITION

They came to Capernaum. When he was in the house, he asked them, "What were you arguing about on the road?" But they kept quiet because on the way they had argued about who was the greatest. Sitting down, Jesus called the Twelve and said, "Anyone who wants to be first must be the very last, and the servant of all."

Mark 9:33–35

"Doree, can you hear me?"

"Yes, where are you?" she asked.

"Inside Afghanistan on a satellite phone."

"Are you safe—everything okay?"

"Yeah, we just drove nine or ten hours on stony riverbeds to avoid land mines, so I'm really beat. But I needed to hear your voice. Are the girls all right?"

"Everyone's good. Are those gunshots I'm hearing?"

"Yeah, we can see some shelling in the distance, on another ridge, but we're safe. Please tell the girls I love them and miss them."

"I will, but don't take any risks."

"I love—"

The signal cut out and I quickly jumped back into our jeep. It probably wasn't wise to be standing on the side of the road anyway. It was littered with abandoned tanks and military equipment.

Earlier in the day, we visited a village atop one of the steep mountains, where children were standing in snow without shoes. The village chief pointed to a slope dotted with mounds of dirt. It was where they buried their children who had died of malnutrition and disease.

We pledged to provide food, clothing, and seed, but I couldn't shake the nightmarish images of those grave sites. They made me want to embrace Doree and the girls and not let go. Many days I felt like an absentee father. This was one of them.

When I was a young boy, every time I'd marched to the plate in Little League, my father stood to his feet and clapped. He'd yell from the bleachers, "Watch the ball hit the bat. Take a level swing. You can do it." But after his death, I walked to the plate in silence. I'd glance at the stands, trying to remember better days. But now, there was no one there. I knew what it was like to be without my father—and so did *my* children.

So much of my life consisted of bouncing from one hotel to the next, where feelings of loneliness set in. I resorted to filling the time with phone calls, emails, television, reading, and prayer. But it wasn't home. There were no substitutes for hugs from my girls or curling up with Doree to watch her favorite TV show, *M*A*S*H*.

Each night on the road, I grappled with my longing to be with my family and my calling to help the poor and suffering. I needed to be there to dry my daughters' tears, but I wanted to do the same for impoverished children around the world. "God," I prayed, "while I'm doing your work, protect my girls. And give Doree strength to manage them without me." The pangs of separation subsided during daylight, but at night they returned with a vengeance.

By now, I had learned not to be seduced by every ministry opportunity or to base major decisions solely on what *I* wanted to do. It was important to give God a vote. As my daughter Erin-Rae says, "God wants our heart more than our works." Nevertheless, sometimes good causes lured me onto airplanes when my wife and children needed my love and attention as well. It was just easier to tell myself *God needs me to travel to the Philippines to feed hungry children* than *I'm staying home because Doree needs me to chauffeur the kids to a soccer game.*

> Sometimes duty and desire clash, and we have to lay aside our preconceptions and pray for the Holy Spirit to guide our decisions.

There's no formula for discerning how to spend our time and resources. Sometimes duty and desire clash, and we have to lay aside our preconceptions and pray for the Holy Spirit to guide our decisions.

Unnecessary Sacrifices

What drives you? It's a common question, but pause and think about it from this angle: Are you led by personal desire or godly duty, or do you fall somewhere in between? Does it depend on the day? On your circumstances? On your ambition and aspirations?

When we follow our own desires, we ask, "What do I want to do?" When we are led by godly duty, we ask, "How is God asking me to partner with him?" I'm not suggesting our interests, plans, and goals are irrelevant to God. Much of who we are and what we care about stems from our Creator. And sometimes what we're passionate about will align with what God is asking of us. But sometimes God asks us to lay our desires down so we can pick up his desires. On occasion, he may ask you and me to postpone a meeting or delay a purchase, for example, so we can fulfill his plans. Many times, God's answer isn't no—it's *not yet*. And, for some, not yet is a tough pill to swallow.

As a journalism student at San Jose State University, I took a creative writing class. The professor's first writing assignment was an essay entitled, "Where I Hope to Be at Age Fifty." I wrote that I wanted to earn a Pulitzer Prize for journalism and serve in public office. Well, I never came close to the Pulitzer. But I was once asked to consider a run for a congressional seat, with assurances I'd be among the frontrunners. Although Doree and I loved the work of Convoy of Hope and felt called to its mission, we'd promised the Lord we would remain open to his plan. The idea of serving the people of our state and making a difference in Washington, DC, was intriguing. We established an exploratory committee and began making the rounds to various district precincts. After much prayer and consultation, we sensed God was asking us to lay down any aspirations for public service to fulfill our duty with Convoy of Hope. Once that decision was made, we never looked back.

In Acts 23:1, the apostle Paul stands before the Sanhedrin in Jerusalem and says, "I have fulfilled my duty to God in all good conscience to this day." It wasn't his passion or personal desire that led him to Jerusalem to face persecution. He wasn't on a career path or chasing a new opportunity. He was motivated by one thing: his duty to God.

Paul understood that living in obedience often requires personal sacrifice—but certainly not all the time. Just because something is sacrificial doesn't make it God's will. And just because you're willing to make a sacrifice doesn't mean your family and friends should too. It's possible to take sacrifice and selflessness to extremes, where you're making unwise decisions and inviting personal injury. Common sense and self-care are still critical pieces of the equation.

When making sacrifices for God, consider these questions:

1. What do I want to do?
2. What is my motivation?
3. What is God asking me to do?
4. What effect will my decision have on my life and others?

My travel calendar was driven by a desire to meet the needs of a myriad of hungry children and hurting families. Before hitting the road, seldom did I ask God for his permission or blessing. I was fulfilling my duty to the poor, so I assumed I had his approval. But sometimes we confuse our desires for God's expectations. We assume duties and burdens he hasn't assigned to us. The mission and outcomes may be noble, but the price we pay is not one he's required. He has called us to do some things, but not everything. He doesn't want us to sacrifice our family or our health, for example, to fulfill our duty. Instead, he wants you and me to stop long enough to ask, "God, what are you asking me to do? How do you want me to do it? When and where are you asking me to do it?"

Doree and the girls claimed I took selflessness and servant-hood to an extreme. In drive-thru lines, for example, they knew they better have their order ready by the time I reached the loudspeaker because I took "drive-thru" literally. I didn't want the car behind us to have to wait longer than ninety seconds. If the girls didn't have their order ready, they knew I'd place one for them. And when I did, I typically ordered enough food for at least two families. I was trying to be so considerate of the cars behind me that I was inconsiderate of the people in *my* car.

Self-Destruction

Compassion is a feel-good word. It conjures up feelings of hope and sacrificial service. But Jesus commands us to go be-yond occasional acts of kindness to another level of compas-sion called *selflessness*. Whereas compassion can be an event or activity, selflessness is a lifestyle of service to others. Jesus was selfless, but he wasn't self-destructive. On occasion, in my quest to be selfless I made sacrifices that crossed the line: speaking at a conference when fighting a high fever, driving an old and unreliable car to avoid reproach, refusing a gift because I thought it was too expensive, choosing not to set the record straight when unfairly criticized. I equated personal sacrifice with selflessness, and selflessness with Christlikeness.

I assumed the more I sacrificed, the more like Jesus I was becoming. But selflessness in the extreme strongly resembles pride or martyrdom. Yes, I was driven by the mission, but at times my personal sacrifice became a badge of honor rather than a quiet offering to God.

I'm not certain when kindness and sacrifice became major themes in my life, but I remember the benevolence shown to my family following my parents' accident. People in our church wrapped their arms around us and showed they cared. As a result, they steered us away from a life of bitterness. I've never forgotten the power of their kindness. It restored my dignity and kept my hope alive. Years later, I found fulfillment in repaying their kindness by helping others. My motives were pure, but I wasn't doing enough to care for myself along the way. While traveling around the globe, eating properly was a challenge. And, at home, exercising regularly was a chore after a long day at the office or an extended road trip. I felt caught in a whirlpool without the inner strength and stamina to swim to safety. Perhaps you're shaking your head right now because you can relate to these ongoing challenges. Hopefully it's heartening to know you are not alone.

Ambition and Happiness

In my experience, when you're raised poor, you feel like a second-class citizen. At times your shoes are tattered, your hair is unkempt, your apartment is small, and your family car is on its last leg. As a kid, I told myself, *Someday, I won't be poor anymore.* That objective compelled me to work hard so I could escape poverty and ascend to a place of abundance and opportunity. Success and respect were the destination, and I assumed ambition would take me there. But unbridled ambition is like a drug. It promises happiness and fulfillment—until you arrive and discover how meaningless fame and fortune are without a selfless purpose. There's nothing wrong with success or abundance as long as you are in the will of God and aren't bent on spending it *all* on yourself.

> Unbridled ambition is like a drug. It promises happiness and fulfillment—until you arrive and discover how meaningless fame and fortune are without a selfless purpose.

Because of my desire to escape my poor upbringing and my desire to help others, I possessed plenty of ambition. But that ambition became an enemy to self-care. It wasn't just compassion and selflessness that compelled me to be a globe-trotter. I was also determined to rise above my past and build a large-scale work. But I confused growth with greatness and promotion with advancement.

Ambition can drive you to make sacrifices God isn't asking you to make. Furthermore, when primarily motivated by ambition, you assume God is at work on your behalf because you appear to be making progress. But in reality, he's sitting this one out. In other words, you can make strides relying on your ability and leveraging your network, but his Spirit can be far from you.

Being driven by reckless ambition doesn't only harm us; the kingdom of God suffers too. When we are consumed by our pursuits, it erodes unity, and our collective mission takes a backseat to competition. The disciples exhibited this same propensity for self-promotion in Mark 9:33–37, when they argued over who among them was the greatest. Jesus was displeased because the disciples

- created conflict by asking an unnecessary question.
- lost their team concept, prioritizing personal goals over their collective mission.
- tried to deceive him by withholding the true nature of their conversation.

Some believers are essentially posing the same question today. Which one of us is the greatest? Which church or charity is the greatest? Which pastor or speaker is the greatest?

Frankly, why do we care who is the greatest when people around the world are suffering and billions don't know Jesus loves them? Reckless ambition takes us in the wrong direction —away from our mission—at the expense of our spiritual health. It shuns humility and grabs for glory when there is only One who deserves our praise, and his name is Jesus.

The hearts of the people who make up a church, ministry, or business are the foundation God builds upon. When our hearts are divided or we have unaddressed character weaknesses, God will only build so tall. Otherwise the organization will collapse under the weight of its own ego. For some individuals and organizations, the mission is right but the foundation is flawed. When the heart is conflicted between personal and missional ambition, the organization suffers. But when the objective is to draw closer to Jesus and to align our goals with his, there's no limit to what he can accomplish.

God had to change our focus from merely building an organization to becoming a channel through which he could bless others. In other words, rather than asking how to grow Convoy of Hope, we asked, "How much can we give away?" That perspective repositioned the organization directly under God's spigot, and we were subsequently drenched in his favor. Resources and opportunities began to flow in our direction as a heart of generosity—rather than a spirit of ambition—propelled the organization. But we also learned God's favor can't be measured by financial statements or name recognition. Many people, churches, businesses, and charities in the center of God's will still face significant challenges. God's favor does not inoculate us against hardship.

As we made adjustments to Convoy of Hope's focus and saw the footprint of the organization grow, we became more aware of the consequences of self-centered ambition and misguided sacrifice. We garnered a fresh understanding of the importance of guarding one's heart and making sure it's in the right place. When your heart and mission are in alignment—and you invite God to call the shots—you become more efficient and your stress levels subside as well. You discover you don't need to strive to create momentum. Instead, you can invite momentum by pursuing a heart after God and repeating a simple prayer like this one: "God, I've tried to *make* things happen. Give me the trust and patience to *let* things happen. I've tried it my way for a long time. Now, I'm ready to do it your way."

Change Survey

Whether you lead an organization or a small family, answer the following questions, which may help you evaluate your current course and make lifestyle changes.

1. How much uninterrupted time do I spend with Jesus and the Word of God each day?
2. How much time am I spending with my family each week?
3. Are my sleep patterns helping me thrive or merely keeping me alive?
4. Is regular physical exercise part of my weekly routine?
5. Am I participating in a local church?
6. What foods or drinks do I use to cope with stress?
7. What forms of entertainment distract me from my work and worries?
8. How much time am I investing in others?

Changes took place in my life when I became serious about time management. Over the course of a week, I conducted an audit to gauge how I was spending my time. I discovered I had more discretionary time at my disposal than I realized. I just needed to substitute the important for the unimportant, which would provide me more time for God, family, friends, and myself. I wish I could say I've mastered the art of self-care, but I am still on the journey. Nevertheless, here are some practical changes I've made for a more balanced life:

1. My sleep became more consistent; I committed to going to bed by 10:30 p.m.
2. I reduced my number of weekend speaking commitments.
3. My dinner appointments were pushed to lunch.
4. I had nutritionists review my diet to assist me in losing weight and gaining more energy.

5. I began to schedule an annual doctor's appointment to monitor any changes to my health.
6. I reassigned some of my responsibilities and projects to coworkers.
7. I've made nightly walks with my wife more frequent.

Running on "E"

A self-professed workaholic and financially successful businessperson confided to me that he was "running on empty." He said he was squandering opportunities for his company and finding only limited time with his family. I asked if he was prepared to make lifestyle changes to restore some sanity to his life. He replied, "Well, it depends on what those changes would be." His response told me all I needed to know. He was so driven by ambition, he couldn't see he was harming himself and those around him. Essentially, his talent was being wasted.

A similar conversation is found in Matthew 19. A rich young ruler approaches Jesus, asking, "Teacher, what good thing must I do to get eternal life?" (v. 16). Jesus instructs him to obey these commandments: "Do not murder, do not commit adultery, do not steal, do not give false testimony, honor your father and mother, and love your neighbor as yourself" (vv. 18–19 NET). The young man claims he has complied with the laws and asks what he still lacks. Jesus replies, "Go, sell your possessions, and give to the poor, and you will have treasure in heaven. Then come, follow me" (v. 21). When he learns Jesus's terms, the young man turns and walks away sad.

Jesus was asking the young man for more than money. He didn't need his money. He was asking him to make significant life changes. In this instance, Jesus was neither speaking against wealth nor speaking up for the poor. Instead, he wanted the young man to revise his priorities and choose a life of generosity. When he peered into the young man's soul, he saw a life consumed by the wrong things. For the rich young ruler, life was more about what he could get than what he could give. That's why Jesus said, "Surrender your possessions and come follow me." The young man walked away with nothing because he wasn't willing to give away something. The rich young ruler clung to his money and his career path and missed out on the greatest investment opportunity of his life.

For me to move into the flow of God's blessings, I had to make some changes and lay down some ambitions. He may be asking you to let go of something as well, so you can receive what he has planned for you. It's highly unlikely Jesus is asking you to empty your bank account and give away all your possessions. But he may be encouraging you to give up a dream car, a relationship, a career path, or even an overly demanding work schedule. Be honest with yourself: if you're nervous about letting go of something, don't let fear tighten your grip. God's blessings far exceed anything you currently own or want. Ask him to help you let go.

Like my business friend, you may be one of millions running on empty. A recent survey by the APA titled "Stress in America 2022" reported the results that "around three-quarters of adults (76%) said they have experienced health impacts due to stress in the prior month." It's not surprising that stress influences our day-to-day functioning, "with more than a quarter [of respondents] (27%) saying that most days they are so stressed they can't function."[1]

Regardless of your stress level and circumstances, the most important step you can take is to invite Jesus to be Chief Operations Officer of your life. Put him in charge of your daily schedule, work activity, leisure time, health, family, finances, and more. Make serving him your primary ambition. Following Jesus comes down to two simple questions: What is he asking you to do, and what are you going to do about it? Determining how to care for yourself and deal with stress becomes clearer—though not necessarily *easier*—when you're doing what Jesus asks you to do.

> Following Jesus comes down to two simple questions: What is he asking you to do, and what are you going to do about it?

Donald P. Coduto, professor of geotechnical engineering at California State Polytechnic University, says, "The most important thing is to keep the most important thing the most important thing."[2] So, when we align ourselves with the ways of Jesus, we can better identify and filter for what is most important.

Jesus doesn't want you to be victimized by stress and worry. Philippians 4:6–7 says,

> Don't fret or worry. Instead of worrying, pray. Let petitions and praises shape your worries into prayers, letting God know your concerns. Before you know it, a sense of God's wholeness, everything coming together for good, will come and settle you down. It's wonderful what happens when Christ displaces worry at the center of your life. (MSG)

Jesus died on a cross so you and I might have eternal life *forever* and abundant life right now. That may not equate to vast wealth, social status, or a shorter to-do list, but Jesus is our passcode to peace and provides the power to overcome life's obstacles. It's important to remember that abundant living isn't life without stop signs or guardrails. Rather, it's a road with stoplights regulated by Jesus for our benefit.

Sometimes it's difficult to break free from the chains of one's circumstances. In fact, you may feel like the enemy has a hold on you and won't let go. Ephesians 4:27 says, "Do not give the devil a foothold." The term *foothold* can be defined as "a situation in which someone has obtained the power or influence needed to get what is wanted."[3] The enemy is always looking for an opening, and by your actions and attitudes you can give him just enough room to gain ground and cause damage. For example, reckless ambition, unforgiveness, envy, pride, greed, self-pity, slothfulness, busyness, ambition, loneliness, and more can become a foothold and cause you to take a step backward.

If you feel you have given the enemy a foothold, here are some suggested next steps:

1. **Keep resisting.** Once the enemy has lost a foothold in your life, he will work hard to regain it. You must continue to resist the enemy by making good decisions and pursuing more of Jesus. James 4:7 says, "Resist the devil, and he will flee from you."
2. **Find strength in numbers.** Consult a pastor, mentor, or trusted friend. Seek their counsel and ask them

to pray for you. Proverbs 11:14 says, "Where there is no guidance, a people falls, but in an abundance of counselors there is safety" (ESV).

3. **Compile a detailed list.** Zoom in on specific, achievable changes you want to make. If, for example, you want to be set free from resentment or unforgiveness, break it down into next steps. That could include asking a friend to partner with you in prayer, seeking counseling, and more.

4. **Give yourself grace.** Rarely are spiritual journeys straight lines. Often they include unexpected turns. When it feels like you are sputtering, give yourself grace. Self-shaming isn't necessary or productive. Simply talk to God and ask him to help you make a comeback. That's what King David did in Psalm 51:10–12, praying: "Create in me a pure heart, O God, and renew a steadfast spirit within me. Do not cast me from your presence or take your Holy Spirit from me. Restore to me the joy of your salvation and grant me a willing spirit, to sustain me."

When my life was a whirlwind of obligation, misguided ambition, and constant stress, I felt like I had fallen into a spiritual rut and didn't know how to claw my way out. At times, my prayers felt like empty words; it was apparent the enemy had gained a foothold. My disappointment in others, my doubts and fears about the future, and my heavy workload threatened to steal my joy. I was following Jesus, but I longed to feel his strong presence again. Something was missing—I needed a spiritual breakthrough.

I was scheduled to participate in a writer's conference and made plans to connect with an editor friend, Lee Grady. One night, he suggested we skip the evening session and spend some time praying together. We met up after dinner in my hotel room. After chatting a while about our families and our desire for more of Jesus, we prayed for one another.

Without warning, it was as if the room was hit by a bolt of lightning. For the next several hours—as what felt like electricity flowed through our bodies in waves—we asked Jesus to bring us healing, understanding, courage, direction, and more. I also asked the Lord to refresh my soul and forgive me for my failures. Desperately I prayed, "Jesus, I'm weary. I'm dry in my spirit. I need more of you."

It was after midnight when I phoned Doree to convey what had happened. My voice was quivering, but I wanted to assure her everything was going to be okay. Jesus had healed some wounds, filled me with indescribable joy, and given me a new level of compassion.

Lee and I camped out in our rooms for the next two days, because the waves of electricity hadn't subsided. We didn't think it was sensible to be sitting in seminars with our hands trembling. I've never since had an experience like that, though I've felt God's presence in other ways. That night strengthened my faith and changed the trajectory of my life.

You don't need to seek an encounter like the one Lee and I had to find healing and direction. Nor do you need to put yourself at risk by making misguided sacrifices or

73

recklessly chasing ambition. Instead, as it says in James 4:8, "Come near to God and he will come near to you." If you are feeling spiritually dry, rest assured Jesus is standing by. He's just waiting to hear you say, "I need your help—I need more of you."

4

THE PROBLEM
WITH SUCCESS

Jesus replied, "Foxes have dens to live in, and birds have
nests, but the Son of Man has no place even to lay his head."

Matthew 8:20 NLT

A steak dinner at the governor's mansion is a few notches
above getting a Big Mac at McDonald's. That's not a
knock on McDonald's, but typically fast-food restaurants
don't offer linen tablecloths and butlers in tuxedos. Tomorrow morning, I'd speak at Missouri's annual prayer breakfast to a banquet hall filled with elected officials, appointed
judges, university presidents, and more. But tonight afforded
an opportunity for our family to dine alone with the governor and first lady.

On the drive to Jefferson City, Doree and I lectured the girls on proper etiquette. We discussed everything from which fork to use to following protocol when greeting our distinguished hosts. We even suggested "safe" talking points. Nonetheless, we feared our oldest daughter, Lindsay, might go rogue and seize the opportunity to share her views on climate change and animal cruelty. She was on her way to law school, so she wasn't short on opinions. During the meal, Erin-Rae, Lauren, and Haly were model citizens, but I could see Lindsay was fighting the temptation to lobby the governor.

Fortunately, the governor—and not Lindsay—led the dinner conversation that evening, inquiring about Convoy of Hope's work in Missouri and hot spots around the world. He wanted to know what his office could do to expand our efforts in the state and expedite disaster response following tornadoes, floods, and ice storms.

It was a memorable evening for our family, but the last few years had proven to be remarkable for Convoy of Hope: the president of the United States conducted a press conference in front of our trucks at a disaster site; Hollywood actors and professional athletes filmed endorsements for us; major corporations donated truckloads of food and supplies; the Super Bowl and other sporting events invited us to conduct high-profile community outreaches; television and radio programs requested interviews and featured Convoy of Hope field reports; and thousands of churches, businesses, civic groups, and individuals linked arms with us to serve the poor and suffering. The organization was experiencing unprecedented growth and notoriety. Millions across the country and around the world were being helped.

One night I was awakened from an unusual dream. I dreamed I was talking with members of a popular pop band. In the dream, I told them God had given them an amazing platform, and they could use it for themselves or use it to feed hungry children around the world. They replied that they wanted to feed hungry children. The next day, with the help of a Convoy team member, I wrote a letter to the band, requesting an opportunity to share about our work around the world. It was a long shot, but I figured we had nothing to lose. Fifty-year-old men like me don't ordinarily dream about pop stars—maybe God was opening a door.

A short time later, we received a phone call from their manager, informing us that the band was FedExing us a large donation, and they wanted to meet with us. So, weeks later, we found ourselves sitting in the front row at a concert in a sea of screaming teenage girls. It was a magical night, other than being blasted by a foam machine from stage. It was a pleasure meeting the band members in the green room and thanking them. Despite their fame and musical success, they exhibited unusual kindness and humility. They genuinely desired to use their platform to help people in need. And other celebrities and professional athletes were offering to help us too. It was as if God had flipped a switch.

Touching the Glory

Make no mistake, success is more dangerous than failure. It's harder to remain humble when you're experiencing momentum and everything appears to be going your way. Success attracts the enemy's attention. He entices us with promises of recognition and urges us to take the credit, climb atop a pedestal, and absorb all the accolades. But he doesn't advertise his methods—he's subtle and covert. Maybe you recognize thoughts like these:

- *I'm not getting full of myself—I just want credit given where credit is due.*
- *Those people shouldn't talk to me that way. They don't know who I am.*
- *I paid my dues, and now it's someone else's turn to do the "grunt work."*
- *They need God's help more than I do.*

The enemy wants us to exalt ourselves and seek the praises of others, because he knows what will follow: "The stuck-up fall flat on their faces" (Prov. 11:2 MSG). As James 4:6 says, "God opposes the proud but shows favor to the humble." It doesn't get much clearer than that. Jesus calls out religious elitists, ambitious disciples, and tight-fisted oppressors in Matthew 23:4–7:

> [The religious scholars and Pharisees] seem to take pleasure in watching you stagger. . . . Their lives are perpetual fashion shows, embroidered prayer shawls one day and flowery prayers the next. They love to sit at the head table at church dinners, basking in the most prominent positions, preening in the radiance of public flattery, receiving honorary degrees, and getting called "Doctor" and "Reverend." (MSG).

God warns that pride is destructive and divisive. Arrogance is poison—for individuals and institutions. At first the symptoms appear harmless. But, left untreated, the poison proves deadly. Pride emerges in shadowy ways: team members find it difficult to celebrate another's success, they openly boast about their achievements, they criticize a coworker to gain advantage, and more.

For Convoy of Hope to survive its success, I knew we needed to establish a foundation of humility and reliance on God. In some ways, it was easier to place our faith in him when resources were

> God warns that pride is destructive and divisive. Arrogance is poison—for individuals and institutions.

scarce and no one knew our name. Even a small measure of success can lead to a false sense of security. The moment you think you're self-sufficient—you're not.

It wasn't enough for me to champion humility and issue warnings about arrogance. As CEO, I needed to model servant leadership—and so did every other leader at Convoy of Hope. Organizational health expert Patrick Lencioni says, "Leadership involves suffering, and it is lonely. . . . It involves the willingness to sacrifice for others, and there are not many people in the world who want to do that."[1]

Along with our organization's success came increased scrutiny. Because of our desire to honor God by operating with integrity, we made accountability and proper governance a high priority. If you do the right thing, the right way, you have God and truth on your side. Hide-and-seek is a child's game, and it shouldn't be standard operating practice for charities, churches, or businesses. When we betray public trust, undesirable consequences soon follow. People might question your judgment or motives, but don't make naive decisions that give them reason to doubt your integrity. For example, be accountable for how well you steward God's resources, measure outcomes, truthfully report results, and avoid making comparisons to other organizations or churches.

Success is dangerous, but not simply because it invites scrutiny. Success can change you, your business, and your organization. For example:

- You begin to think you're more special than others.
- You believe the positive things people say about you and immediately reject the negative.
- You forget to seek God's opinion—you believe you have things well under control.
- You assume credit for successes with an occasional nod in God's direction.
- You stop abiding by the principles that led to your success.
- You are quick to share your opinion with others but ignore their critiques.
- You become careless with God's resources.
- You begin evaluating people and relationships based on what they can do for you and whether they will propel you forward.
- You become more focused on what you have built than on how to effectively fulfill your mission.
- You live for winning the approval of others rather than bringing pleasure to the Creator.
- You tell yourself the end result justifies questionable methods.

Requests for Help

Convoy of Hope's meteoric growth ushered in a fresh set of organizational challenges. Daily, we received emails requesting aid from around the globe: famine in Africa, typhoons in the Philippines, tornadoes in Kansas, flooding in New York, fires in California, community outreaches in Chicago, refugees in Bosnia, and more. Unfortunately, our resources didn't come anywhere near to catching up with the human need.

When requests poured in, our goal was to respond with a yes or a maybe. But now we were having to say no or not now far too often. I was tortured by our inability to respond immediately. In many cases, if we didn't deliver food, I knew it meant children would be forced to scavenge from garbage heaps, beg in the streets, or sniff glue to take away their hunger. As UNICEF reports, "nearly half of all deaths in children under five are attributable to undernutrition."[2]

Meanwhile, in parts of Africa and Southeast Asia, extremists were buying the allegiance of children for a bowl of rice and a cup of water. In Somalia, a 2022 article by the Foreign Policy Research Institute tells us,

> Given the current socioeconomic status of many Somalis and the lack of economic opportunity in the agricultural sector, [the country's terrorist group] may become more enticing for individuals with limited opportunities. The [group's] recruits are as young as fourteen, and 70 percent are younger than 24 years old. In Somalia, where the median age is 17 years old, recruitment trends are a cause for concern.[3]

As far as I was concerned, it was *all* unacceptable. Some nights, I couldn't sleep as tears soaked my pillow. The odor of failure was stronger than the smell of success. We had to find a way to do more.

As we attempted to expand the organization's infrastructure, it was apparent we were lacking key personnel. We needed to attract additional team members who could take Convoy of Hope to the next level. Internationally, we needed more in-country leaders with expertise in nutrition, agronomy, spiritual development, education, and business. In the States, we needed additional field representatives, food procurement directors, outreach coordinators, truck drivers, and communications specialists. To accomplish the task before us, we had critical holes to fill. I felt the gravity of those personnel decisions because millions of lives were at stake.

Leaders must discern whether an applicant is a potential world changer who fits the culture or a lawsuit waiting to happen. In interviews, it's easy to be impressed by a person's talent and charisma. But those attributes are less important than their faith, character, and chemistry. Talent can be taught and personality developed, but poor character and a lack of chemistry are deal breakers.

The biggest mistakes I've made as a leader relate to hiring people who couldn't adapt to the culture. In some cases, they began with great promise but later it proved to be the wrong fit. Early in Convoy of Hope's history, I found departures disconcerting. I wanted everyone to get along, find fulfillment, and be part of the family. But, after taking it on the chin a few times, I discovered some departures were God's way of protecting the organization and its mission.

Assembly Required

As a leadership team, we sensed God wanted to entrust Convoy of Hope with more for one reason: he wanted to do more. But without the necessary funds, it would be impossible to assemble the right team. We made a covenant to fast and to pray daily for God's provision. Some mornings, I closed the blinds to my office and locked the door. Kneeling at my chair, I asked Jesus to perform miracles: "I know you want to reach the poor and suffering more than we do. We're willing to go and serve them, but we need your help," I prayed. "We can't do this without more of you, more resources, *and* more workers."

Years earlier—at a time I believed God was extending the reach of Convoy of Hope—I presented him with a shopping list. I wrote four words on a sticky note and prayed over it for weeks. The four words were *trucks*, *warehouses*, *food*, and *finances*. I quickly discovered that God is a good reader, for he did the impossible. He provided a fleet of tractor-trailers, opened doors to warehouses, introduced us to suppliers, and sent us new partners. If it had worked once, I deemed it was worth trying again. So I presented God with a second shopping list, this time consisting of personnel needs. I tucked a copy in my Bible and began calling out the names of each position in prayer. God was listening. Within months, he helped us check off every position on the list. He sent people with the right hearts and skill sets and provided donations to underwrite the additional payroll. God was at work. He had already written a script for Convoy of Hope. Now we just needed to make sure we followed it.

To reinforce the organization's core values, emphasize corporate prayer, and foster a spirit of unity, we gathered as a team on Wednesday mornings. That weekly session galvanized the workforce and helped assimilate newcomers. When a team is in sync—pursuing the same objectives and speaking with one voice—there's no limit to what God can accomplish. But if a team isn't flowing together, God's blessings aren't flowing either. I'm certain team members grew weary of hearing me speak week after week about humility, unity, and compassion. But, despite our recent success, I knew the organization was still fragile. Convoy of Hope would rise or fall on whether we embraced the wisdom of Proverbs 11: "When pride comes, then comes disgrace, but with humility comes wisdom. The integrity of the upright guides them, but the unfaithful are destroyed by their duplicity. . . . A generous person will prosper; whoever refreshes others will be refreshed" (vv. 2–3, 25).

The aim of the board of directors and team members was for Convoy of Hope to reflect our love for Jesus and his love for people. But that meant we had to go beyond building an image to earning a reputation. Ecclesiastes 7:1 says, "A good reputation is more valuable than costly perfume" (NLT). For the organization to earn a favorable reputation, we had to honor our word, underpromise and overdeliver, and operate at the highest level of excellence and integrity.

Based on our stated objectives and the principles espoused in our Wednesday gatherings, we prepared the following as a statement of core values:

- **Love**: we love others unconditionally, as God loves us.
- **Dignity**: we recognize and respect the worth of every person, serving all as guests of honor.

- **Service**: we honor God by serving others and expecting nothing in return.
- **Excellence**: we strive for quality in all we do to bring glory to God.
- **Integrity**: we live and serve in a manner that is above reproach.
- **Unity**: we build bridges across denominational, ethnic, and socioeconomic lines, believing unity is essential to having God's blessing.
- **Support**: we assist local congregations and groups, believing they are often best positioned to serve the needs of their communities.
- **Partnership**: we build collaborative relationships, believing we can do more together than we can do apart.
- **Hope**: we give people confidence that God sees their need and wants to provide direction and purpose for their lives.
- **Advocacy**: we are a passionate voice for those in need, encouraging others to respond to the biblical mandate to remember the poor.

At times, Convoy of Hope loosely resembled a Silicon Valley start-up. Having graduated from San Jose State University, which is near the high-tech epicenter, I was familiar with the chaos that can accompany a growing business. Typically, start-ups require long workdays, recruit highly sought-after talent, tackle big problems, expand quickly, dive into global markets, and invest in research and development. They want to be the first to recognize and capitalize on market trends.

They aren't afraid to redefine success, reestablish the target, or redirect their course. And each employee shares responsibility for the company's quarterly numbers.

With new opportunities, new faces, and new name recognition, Convoy of Hope was forced to mature quickly—much like a start-up. The growth also forced me to sharpen my peripheral vision and be more strategic in my decision-making. I also discovered my words and actions had a ripple effect. People were quick to repeat what I said and pass along my opinions—even when I was wrong. I had to become more measured in my communication.

Unless leaders remain grounded in God and his Word, we can find ourselves in a heady and perilous place. Despite success, we have a responsibility to work at making sure people don't place us on a pedestal. Pedestals are dangerous places—they are potential diving platforms. Proverbs 16:18 says, "Pride goes before destruction, a haughty spirit before a fall." There's only One who belongs on a pedestal. His name is Jesus, and he traded his throne in heaven for a cross.

Iron Sharpens Iron

Regardless of our job, title, or calling, we all need genuine friendships. God created us that way. With greater responsibility at home or work comes greater risk. We need a circle of friends who help us remain reliant on the Lord and make Christ-honoring decisions. Proverbs 27:17 says, "As iron sharpens iron, so one person sharpens another."

True friends endeavor to serve. They're eager to listen and come to your defense. They tell you what you need to hear when it's the last thing you want to hear. They know when to remain silent and when to offer sound advice. You can trust they have your best interest at heart, because they've proven it time and again.

At the Last Supper, Jesus demonstrated servanthood and true friendship to his disciples. On the night he was betrayed, he removed his outer garment and took a towel and a basin of water and washed their feet. This was

> **True friends endeavor to serve. They tell you what you need to hear when it's the last thing you want to hear.**

not intended to be a celebratory banquet. It was the beginning of Jesus's walk to the cross. And yet he wanted to leave behind a message to his disciples on the importance of serving one another. In Matthew 20:26–28, Jesus says,

> The greatest one among you will live as the one who is called to serve others, because the greatest honor and authority is reserved for the one with the heart of a servant. For even the Son of Man did not come expecting to be served but to serve and give his life in exchange for the salvation of many. (TPT)

After washing the disciples' feet, Jesus reveals to Peter that he will betray him three times. Jesus listens to Peter's denials and says, "But I have prayed for you, Simon [Peter], that your faith may not fail. And when you have turned back, strengthen your brothers" (Luke 22:32). Note that Jesus didn't ask Peter to pay a fine or suffer punishment for his betrayal. Instead, he tells him to serve his brothers.

Let me encourage you to take a long look in the mirror. Has success lured you away from Jesus? Has pride entered your heart and, as a result, you've made mistakes? Are you intoxicated by approval and applause, or is the pressure to succeed suffocating? If so, Jesus wants to help you turn back to him and find true fulfillment. He's not requesting an offering or penance of any kind. He simply wants you to confess your sins and, like Peter, begin looking for opportunities to meet the needs of others and strengthen them in their faith. Make every day a love letter to God by investing in someone's life.

5

"EASY" TARGETS

Then one of the Twelve—the one called Judas Iscariot—
went to the chief priests and asked, "What are you willing
to give me if I deliver him over to you?" So they counted out
for him thirty pieces of silver. From then on Judas watched
for an opportunity to hand him over.

Matthew 26:14–16

It was 2:15 a.m. and I couldn't sleep. After tossing and turning for several hours, I retreated to the kitchen to grab a
snack. Unfortunately, this had become a pattern. Night after
night, food was my sedative of choice. My weight climbed
twenty-five pounds in eight months, and exercise had become
a four-letter word for me. I felt like I was heading into a raging storm and wasn't sure how to change course.

The demands of a growing organization and the wounds
of difficult relationships had taken their toll. Even a brief

sabbatical couldn't heal the hurt inside me. I found relief by praying and reading God's Word, but lasting peace evaded me like our family dog, Connor. After stealing a sock or sneaker, that beagle was impossible to catch.

I was never tempted to turn to alcohol, drugs, or other numbing agents. Despite my inner turmoil, I felt close to Jesus. Eventually, I knew, he would help me navigate the storm raging inside my heart. But this was a spiritual battle on a scale I had never experienced. My family and a few friends were there to offer encouragement, but they could do only so much.

Close Calls

Meanwhile, I continued to fulfill my duties at Convoy of Hope. We were experiencing God's favor, and I was evolving as a leader. Other than those who noticed my weight gain and the bags under my sleep-deprived eyes, most assumed I was on top of the world. But I was merely following the playbook I had learned as a kid: just press on in the face of hardship and disappointment. I kept pushing the pain down, under a mountain of work and responsibility. *It's time for me to persevere—to push through*, I told myself. *God will take care of me if I just keep doing his work.* As some might say, I was white-knuckling it. Later, I discovered that while God will take care of me, he never intends for me to be absent from the equation. He expects me to take adequate care of myself too. I can't go to a personal trainer every week, for example, and take a nap while the trainer does all the work.

At a Convoy of Hope board of directors meeting, in executive session, chairperson Brad Rosenberg asked me a simple question: "Hal, how are you doing?" Measuring my words, I said, "God is doing amazing things through Convoy, but right now it feels like the target on my back is quite large." In a show of love and support, the board members promptly gathered around me to pray. Perhaps they sensed the gravity of the situation—that I was in the throes of intense spiritual warfare. The enemy was going to great lengths to thwart the expansion of Convoy of Hope and wouldn't mind taking me out of the picture altogether.

It had been a strange and unsettling season.

When I was in Japan, responding to the 2011 earthquake and tsunami, my life was nearly cut short. We had taken a bullet train to rendezvous with our relief teams in the affected areas. On our return to Tokyo, we were riding a tall escalator at the train station when a man lost his balance and tumbled from the top. I tried to block his fall, but he hit me with such force that I flew backward. My head hit the edge of the escalator step, and I was knocked out cold. I rode to the top of the escalator on my back. When I finally regained consciousness, paramedics were standing over me. I was taken to the hospital for X-rays and treatment on a six-inch gash. There was no permanent damage, but it took four months for me to fully recover from the concussion.

A month later, I was driving home from my daughter's swim meet on I-44 in Missouri when the semitruck in front of me swerved into the emergency lane. Instinctively, I followed. Seconds later, a car flew by us, driving on the wrong side of the freeway. I locked eyes with the driver, an elderly woman, but it happened so fast I couldn't even lift a hand to warn her. Then I heard a horrifying collision—she hit the car behind me. I circled back to help, but police had already arrived on the scene, and I could hear ambulance sirens in the distance. Three people lost their lives, including the elderly driver.

Several weeks after that accident, I noticed an insect bite on my thigh. The affected area spread rapidly, and I experienced nausea, vomiting, and rashes. Despite my protests, Doree convinced me to consult a doctor. After examining the bite and hearing the symptoms, he surmised I had been bitten by a brown recluse spider, one of the most venomous insects in North America. Although the spider bite was not normally life-threatening, the series of close calls left me feeling like I'd been targeted.

Counseling

Besides fasting and praying on our behalf, members of the board of directors recommended that my family and I spend time with a Christian counselor. I had never confided in a licensed counselor or therapist, so I wasn't sure what to expect. Nonetheless, it sounded like a promising idea. I wish I could have consulted a counselor as a boy, following my father's death.

Two counselors accepted the assignment and, a short time later, we found ourselves meeting with them at a retreat center. Doree and I cried our way through most of the initial session. For the first time, I shared painful memories: how, as a child, I'd battled feelings of inferiority and insecurity, and how I'd felt responsible for the well-being of my mother and siblings.

By the conclusion of our first day, the counselors offered us this valuable advice:

1, Prioritize your emotional, physical, and spiritual health. Develop a plan and stick to it.

2. Tend to your emotional wounds properly, so they don't fester and become more painful.

3. Reduce your workload. Increase sleep and exercise. Do what's important and say no to what isn't.

4. Schedule more leisure and family time into your calendar.

5. Understand that it's okay to step back from quarrelsome people and complicated circumstances. (That may be the most Christlike action you can take.)

6. Forgive adversaries—but that doesn't mean they should be trusted. Trust is earned, and so is distrust. Trusting the wrong people is poor stewardship.

7. You are responsible for *your* character and no one else's. Don't blame yourself for the decisions and mistakes of others.

8. Give yourself a break. Extend to yourself the same grace you believe others deserve and benefit from.

Putting on Armor

With the counselors' help, my recognition of the enemy's arsenal expanded. In spiritual warfare, his weapons include worry, discouragement, depression, loneliness, envy, betrayal, unforgiveness, and more. But when we are consumed with deflecting his attacks, it's impossible to give God our best. Ephesians 6:11 says, "Put on the full armor of God, so that you can take your stand against the devil's schemes." When we are encased in God's armor, we can stand our ground.

We don't need to be preoccupied with the enemy's arrows. The enemy wants us to live on the defensive, always fearful of his next attack. God wants us to mount a counteroffensive of love and compassion in the world, fully trusting his strength and protection.

With the help of God, the counselors, and my family, I stepped into a new set of armor. It began with this simple prayer: "God, I want to make a difference in the world, but I know the enemy wants to prevent me from doing your work. So, I need the full protection of your armor." Then I wrote a list of what was creating stress in my life and placed the promises of God beside each one. I suggest using my example to create your own chart.

You Can Reduce Stress

By putting on the full armor of God, you can march ahead with strong assurance. Here are seven steps that will reduce stress and enhance your life.

1. Get real.

Just because you possess the ability to perform a task, it doesn't mean you've been called to it. God doesn't expect you to go from multitasking to multitude-tasking. He gave you limitations for a reason—so you wouldn't attempt to do everything or rescue everyone.

No matter how hard you try, how smart or dedicated you are, or how compassionate you may be, you still can't control the rain. The rain falls on everyone. This means you can't control the behavior of others or the consequences of their choices. Of course, you want the best for them. You hate to see anyone fall. But not everyone can go where God is taking you. He doesn't expect you to take the garbage strewn across your neighbor's lawn and relocate the trash to *your* lawn. Each person must deal with their own stuff.

2. Speak life.

The enemy wants you to live in a constant state of despair. He perpetuates negativity in your life by making your circumstances appear hopeless and clouding your perspective. Nothing is gained by repeating the lies of the enemy. What are you saying to yourself? Are you quoting the promises of God or echoing the lies of the evil one? Would you speak to a friend the way you speak to yourself? What you say to yourself will determine whether you advance with hope or retreat in fear.

Some of us assume we are experiencing spiritual warfare when we're actually suffering the consequences of our actions. Some people blame the enemy when they should be examining their heart. And sometimes it's not one or the other—you might be able to see how you contributed to the situation you're now in *and* how the enemy is working overtime to trip and trap you. We can avoid playing into the enemy's hands by refusing to resort to gossip, slander, or spreading misinformation. Don't allow yourself to slide down the slope of finding joy in someone else's pain or trouble. When we do that, we're separating ourselves from the heart of Jesus and inviting conflict. What we say about another person affects our ability to hear God's voice and limits what he can do in and through our lives. When we wound others with our words, we bring shame on ourselves. If you want to experience the favor of God, be accountable for the words you speak. James 3:9–10 says, "With the tongue we praise our Lord and Father, and with it we curse human beings, who have been made in God's likeness. Out of the same mouth come praise and cursing. My brothers and sisters, this should not be."

3. Forgive yourself and others.

If, at times, you feel like you've failed yourself, your family, and God—you are not alone. If you have requested his gift of forgiveness, then forgive yourself. There is nothing to be gained by living in regret. That will only steal your joy, drain your strength, and cloud your judgment. Perhaps you feel you don't deserve happiness because of what you did or didn't do. Jesus doesn't agree with you. He died on a cross so you could live free of guilt and shame. That doesn't mean you shouldn't seek to restore, replenish, and provide restitution for your wrongs. But sometimes that isn't possible. You may have to trust Jesus to bring healing to the situation. Meanwhile, he wants you to serve him without looking over your shoulder.

If others have maligned you and attacked your reputation, do yourself a favor and forgive them. Forgiving your perpetrators may not repair the damage they've caused, but it will set you free from the bondage of hatred. Matthew 6:15 says, "But if you do not forgive others their sins, your Father will not forgive your sins." You may be saying right now, "The people who hurt me don't deserve my understanding and forgiveness." They may not, but caring for *yourself* means learning to replace bitterness with enough love that you're willing to pray for your enemies. Matthew 5:44 says, "Love your enemies and pray for those who persecute you."

When adversaries repay your kindness with slander and return your generosity with selfishness, naturally it leaves a bitter taste in your mouth. It hurts. But we choose what our next response will look and sound like. We can invite resentment to take up residence in our heart—or we can walk away knowing we have responded in a Christlike way.

Exercising restraint and giving coworkers, friends, and family members the benefit of the doubt is not always easy. But, like you, there are times I'm grateful I didn't repeat everything aloud I rehearsed in my mind. Biting our tongue can save us a lot of grief. That was the case for me when Doree decided to get her hair permed many years ago. Either her hairdresser was an amateur or she had a really bad day, because Doree walked out of the salon looking like a troll. We were dating at the time, so I chose my words carefully.

"What do you think?" she asked, posing for me.

The word *awful* came to mind, but instead I said, "That's a new look."

"But do you like it?"

"It's good to try different styles," I replied.

"You don't like it, do you?" she asked.

"It's fine—I'll get used to it."

My diplomatic skills were apparently lacking, because she broke up with me a few weeks later. But had I confronted her with the unfiltered truth, I doubt we would have ever gotten back together. Restraint saved my chance at marrying the woman I loved. Proverbs 21:23 says, "Those who guard their mouths and their tongues keep themselves from calamity."

Source of Stress	God's Promise
Difficult People	**Matthew 5:43–46**
	You have heard that it was said, "Love your neighbor and hate your enemy." But I tell you, love your enemies and pray for those who persecute you, that you may be children of your Father in heaven. He causes his sun to rise on the evil and the good, and sends rain on the righteous and the unrighteous. If you love those who love you, what reward will you get? Are not even the tax collectors doing that?
Limited Resources	**Philippians 4:19**
	And my God will meet all your needs according to the riches of his glory in Christ Jesus.
Weariness	**Matthew 11:28–30**
	Come to me, all you who are weary and burdened, and I will give you rest. Take my yoke upon you and learn from me, for I am gentle and humble in heart, and you will find rest for your souls. For my yoke is easy and my burden is light.
Fear of the Future	**Matthew 6:33–34**
	But seek first his kingdom and his righteousness, and all these things will be given to you as well. Therefore do not worry about tomorrow, for tomorrow will worry about itself. Each day has enough trouble of its own.
Fear of Failure	**Philippians 4:13**
	I can do all this through him who gives me strength.
Anger	**Ephesians 4:26–27**
	Go ahead and be angry. You do well to be angry—but don't use your anger as fuel for revenge. And don't stay angry. Don't go to bed angry. Don't give the Devil that kind of foothold in your life. (MSG)
Regret	**2 Corininthians 7:10**
	Godly sorrow brings repentance that leads to salvation and leaves no regret, but worldly sorrow brings death.

4. Go beyond.

The apostle Paul had to move beyond his past. Before his conversion to Christianity, Saul of Tarsus was known as a murderer and slanderer. In Philippians 3:13–14, Paul says,

I'm not saying that I have this all together, that I have it made. But I am well on my way, reaching out for Christ, who has so wondrously reached out for me. Friends, don't get me wrong: By no means do I count myself an expert in all of this, but I've got my eye on the goal, where God is beckoning us onward—to Jesus. I'm off and running, and I'm not turning back. (MSG)

For many years, I thought I had to forgive, forget, and move on. But I've since revised that expectation to forgive, let go, and move forward. You may have such a tight grip on the pain of your past that moving forward feels impossible. Granted, moving beyond a painful past is seldom easy. Fortunately, you don't have to muster *all* the energy to make it happen. You simply need to present to God a willing heart. But whether you travel a millimeter or a mile, it's the forward motion that counts. With Jesus's help, you can rise above your past and serve others. In Philippians 2:3–4, Paul says, "Don't push your way to the front; don't sweet-talk your way to the top. Put yourself aside, and help others get ahead. Don't be obsessed with getting your own advantage. Forget yourselves long enough to lend a helping hand" (MSG).

> For many years, I thought I had to forgive, forget, and move on. But I've since revised that expectation to forgive, let go, and move forward.

5. Choose peace.

Jesus designed us to walk in peace, but that's impossible without seeking unity and choosing forgiveness. As followers of Jesus, we must lead with love rather than judgment and condemnation. Most of all, our words and deeds need to reflect the peace and justice of Jesus.

Growing up in the San Francisco Bay Area, I remember the Vietnam War protests at the University of California, Berkeley, and the hippie culture that emerged out of Haight-Ashbury. It was a restless time, with new fashion, new sexual mores, and rock music sweeping the nation. This time was also a precursor to the Jesus Revolution of the 1970s. Although I was just a welfare kid in a rapidly changing world, one song gave me hope: "They'll Know We Are Christians by Our Love" became an anthem for young people disillusioned with the status quo. They were weary of racism, hatred, gender inequality, poverty, religiosity, materialism, and war. This song could be heard at nightclubs, churches, *and* public protests. One lyric stood out to me: "We will guard each other's dignity and save each man's pride." That is the message of Ephesians 4:3: "Make every effort to keep the unity of the Spirit through the bond of peace." The enemy's strategy is to fill our hearts with selfish words and a contentious spirit. Jesus's response is to fill us with selfless words and unity. He wants us to be known by our love for each other.

Conflict is inevitable. Jesus had numerous confrontations. And not every clash ended like a Hallmark movie. Matthew 5:24 says reconciliation is the desired outcome, but sometimes conflicts can be resolved only with God's help. In Romans 12:18, Paul instructs us to "live at peace with everyone." He includes two important conditions: "if it is possible" and "as far as it depends on you." That leaves a lot less in our hands and more in God's. The Message version says it this way: "Don't insist on getting even; that's not for you to do. 'I'll do the judging,' says God. 'I'll take care of it.'"

6. Be noble.

Every sunrise presents another opportunity to be noble. I'm not alluding to societal ranking or bravery; I'm referring to how one's character is lived out. Paying for someone's meal or complimenting a server for a job well done is kind and can make a big difference. But nobility is absent if you're doing those things to meet a quota or for praise and recognition.

Being a good humanitarian doesn't make you noble.

Being religious doesn't make you noble.

Being famous or admired doesn't make you noble.

Having thousands of congregants or followers on social media doesn't make you noble.

The noble person is one who does the right thing regardless of who's looking (or not looking) and despite personal cost. It is more about a person's ongoing character and integrity than an occasional good deed. In Matthew 23:5–7, Jesus has this to say about the Pharisees and scribes: "Everything they do is done for people to see . . . they love the place of honor at banquets and the most important seats in the synagogues; they love to be greeted with respect in the marketplaces and to be called 'Rabbi' by others."

Jesus modeled nobility. As his follower, if you commit to doing the right thing, time and again you will walk out of the enemy's entrapments and into the favor of God. "Whoever walks in integrity walks securely, but whoever takes crooked paths will be found out. . . . The way of the LORD is a refuge for the blameless, but it is the ruin of those who do evil" (Prov. 10:9, 29).

In the Old Testament, Samuel served as judge and spiritual guardian over Israel. He called his people to purity and devotion to God. In his farewell speech, recorded in 1 Samuel 12, he asks the people five questions: "Whose ox have I taken? Whose donkey have I taken? Whom have I cheated? Whom have I oppressed? From whose hand have I accepted a bribe to make me shut my eyes?" (v. 3). In response, the people confirm that Samuel has been a consistent and credible leader. He earned their trust by putting the needs of others first. Samuel's influence and reputation were a direct result of his character. In the eyes of his people, he was noble. Some people are motivated by selfishness. They do good deeds for all the wrong reasons. They give to get something in return. It's just who they are. They may still be attempting to build their résumés and network in heaven. Samuel, in contrast, was driven by one purpose: his desire to please God. Likewise, the more you seek to bring pleasure to your Creator, the more noble your ways will be.

> **If you commit to doing the right thing, time and again you will walk out of the enemy's entrapments and into the favor of God.**

7. Measure well.

In John 16:33, Jesus says,

"I have told you these things, so that in Me you may have [perfect] peace. In the world you have tribulation and distress and suffering, but be courageous [be confident, be undaunted, be filled with joy]; I have overcome the world." [My conquest is accomplished, My victory abiding.] (AMP).

You may be telling yourself, *That verse works for some people, but my life hasn't played out that way.* God's favor is not measured by how much money you earn, how physically strong you are, how many opportunities you have, what status you've gained, or how famous you've become. His favor is measured by how much of Jesus you have in your life.

When facing the flaming arrows of the enemy, you may feel like an easy target. But nothing could be further from the truth. As a child of God, you are an invincible target. The bullseye on your back may be huge and your enemy's attacks relentless, but you do not need to shudder in fear. You can hold your ground, because God and his angels are standing by to deflect arrows and protect you from harm. Ephesians 6:16 says, "Take up the shield of faith, with which you can extinguish all the flaming arrows of the evil one."

Your faith in God is your shield.

It doesn't take a military expert to understand that shields are designed for the battlefield. They aren't required equipment for those who live in virtual isolation. The shield of faith is needed most by those who take the love of Jesus to a hurting world. When you decide to go beyond your desires and serve the needs of others, you will face opposition from the enemy. When you believe people can be rescued from despair and find hope, flaming arrows will come your way.

And when you envision neighborhoods and villages free of drugs, crime, and poverty—and you help families discover Jesus—the target on your back will grow. But the enemy is simply no match for those, like you and me, who believe Jesus can work through them to bring help and hope to a hurting world.

6

PUSHING RESET

Come with me by yourselves to a quiet place and get some rest.

Mark 6:31

In case you've ever wondered, the Guinness World Record for consecutive visits to a Disney theme park is 2,995 days. A California man dedicated eight years, three months, and thirteen days of his life to hanging out with Mickey Mouse at "the happiest place on earth."

My daughters have a crazy love for theme parks, but I doubt even they'd have an interest in trying to break that record. When my daughter Lindsay was small, I asked her what she was looking forward to the most about heaven. She replied, "Big roller coasters with no waiting lines." She and her sisters learned to squeeze the most fun out of parks like Silver Dollar City and Worlds of Fun. Days in advance, they'd map out their sequence of rides. Even bathroom breaks were synchronized. They'd sprint from one roller coaster to the next, ignoring the tamer rides, exhibits, and stage shows. They were thrill-seekers on a mission, and Doree and I didn't mind going along for the ride—literally.

For our family, amusement parks have always been a fun place to escape day-to-day duties and enjoy being together. We leave our problems in the parking lot. And for twelve hours straight, our focus is on having fun and being together. After such a full day, we exit the park physically exhausted and mentally refreshed. It's not that our problems and obligations disappear but our park tickets are permission slips to prioritize fun and laughter.

That raises an important question: How can we prioritize laughter and gain perspective without spending $2,000 to ride Space Mountain and have a picture taken with Donald Duck? How do we remain refreshed right where we are?

Investing in Happiness

Everyone becomes fatigued, restless, grumpy, and irritable. Feeling that way for sustained periods of time, though, can open the door to depression. When discouragement threatens to become a long-term tenant in your life, you have three options:

1. You can try to **ignore** it.
2. You can **isolate** yourself from others.
3. You can **investigate**. Get curious and try to identify activities that bring you joy and encouragement. You can also investigate what is contributing to your

discouragement through personal reflection or speaking with a Christian counselor.

At first glance, investing in your happiness may strike you as selfish, but it's the only reasonable option. No one wants to live discouraged when they can have a positive outlook. And if you ignore your own happiness, eventually it will negatively affect your life and those around you.

Investing in your own happiness is full of possibilities: reading a book, watching a movie, attending a sporting event, inviting friends to dinner, taking a nap, going for a long walk or bike ride, taking a drive in the country, scrapbooking, crocheting, chasing a golf ball, playing board games, relaxing on the beach, attending a concert or dramatic play, spending time with your church family or small group, gardening, volunteering at a local school or assisted living facility, rock climbing, skiing, and much more.

In other words, grownups need recess too.

Career coach Ashley Stahl says, "It might sound too good to be true, but simply engaging in creative behaviors (even just coloring in those trendy adult coloring books) improves brain function, mental health, and physical health."[1] If you don't know where to start, workers in places like Silicon Valley have discovered the creative benefits of tossing tennis balls in the air, kneading playdough, solving crossword puzzles, playing Ping-Pong, throwing darts, and

> Sometimes work must wait, dishes must go unwashed, and friends need to get over it. Because your mental health and encouragement are simply more important.

more. The particular activity isn't as important as finding a way to bring moments of creativity and play into each day.[2]

Many sabotage their happiness by allowing guilt or fear to prevent them from doing things they love—or *might* love. They tell themselves they shouldn't waste time reading a book or catching rays at the beach because they have a pile of work accumulating on their desk. They cancel plans to attend a concert because they have an unfinished task. Or they talk themselves out of taking a long overdue vacation to attend to an obligation. Sometimes work must wait, dishes must go unwashed, and people need to get over it. Because your mental health and encouragement are simply more important.

Snooze Buttons

When the pandemic reared its ugly head in 2020, my life changed overnight, like it did for many. Members of the Convoy of Hope team began working twelve or more hours a day to respond to the expanding human need in the States and around the world. In the months that followed, more than a thousand churches and tens of thousands of volunteers came together to distribute two hundred million meals to families suddenly unemployed and to children who had lost access to school lunch programs. While political and medical disputes monopolized the news, we had a front row seat to the compassion and generosity of congregations, businesses, partners, and volunteers. It was inspiring to see so many link arms (figuratively speaking) to care for others.

Eighteen months later, when some of the more obvious effects of the pandemic began to fade, like many others I found myself emotionally spent. Separation from friends and coworkers, limited access to church and other venues, a demanding workload, dietary and sleep changes, and a disruption to my exercise routine had left me almost numb. It was obvious I hadn't adequately cared for myself during the pandemic. When I looked in the mirror, I didn't recognize that man with the puffy skin and vacant eyes. For months, I'd woken each morning pondering how we could continue feeding five hundred thousand children each day when global supply chains were at a standstill. My prayer times had become strategy sessions, asking God how to keep our fleet of tractor-trailers crisscrossing the nation. The Convoy of Hope team worked with a sense of urgency, because we knew families and churches were counting on us to deliver truckloads of food and supplies. Failure wasn't an option. But, after so many months of operating in crisis mode, our team was understandably weary and worn. It was the right time to take a "holy pause" to thank God for his protection and provision. Everyone was given several weeks to be with their families and recharge their batteries.

As much as anyone, I needed time to rebound. I didn't like feeling empty and exhausted, especially when hundreds of team members needed to be encouraged and reassured. It was time to stop for a few weeks and push the reset button emotionally, physically, relationally, and spiritually. From time to time, regardless of your state in life, you need opportunity to reset and be refreshed.

Dirt and Debris

In Genesis 26, Isaac finds himself weary and thirsty. He needs to be refreshed. He has a decision to make: he can start digging a hole in hopes that he strikes water, or he can journey to his father's wells. He decides it makes more sense to go where he knows there's water. He travels to the old wells only to discover they have been filled with debris, rubbish, and dirt. But he knows the water is there—he just can't see it. He proceeds to dig out the debris, and that thirst-quenching, life-giving water begins to flow—and he is fully satisfied.

You may have some debris accumulation in your life that is obstructing your view of all God has for you. Now is a good time to examine the condition of your heart and be spiritually refreshed. When circumstances like a pandemic enter one's orbit and create additional pressures, temptations to sin can appear like a Hollywood red carpet. In Joel chapters 1–2, the prophet outlines three steps we can take to leave sin behind, draw nearer to God, and push the reset button so we can live encouraged.

1. **Repent of sin.** With sorrow and regret, we need to trust God with our honesty. He isn't looking for half-hearted prayers. He wants to hear us say, "God, I blew it. I need your help. I gave in to temptation. Forgive me for what I've done and for what I haven't done."

2. **Take action.** Joel instructs us to reposition ourselves under God's authority through fasting and wearing sackcloth. There must be an outward demonstration or visible evidence that reflects the change taking place in our hearts. As it says in Luke 3:8, "Produce fruit in keeping with repentance." It's not enough to talk a big game—to sound spiritual and repentant. Authentic repentance is always followed by changes in attitude and behavior.

Fasting is a visible demonstration that you desire a new beginning. It's like marking a day on your calendar on which you are changing course and placing your future in God's hands. When the book of Joel was written, wearing sackcloth was symbolic of mourning. There was nothing special about a scratchy, uncomfortable garment. It was simply a sign the old was being left behind. Today, God isn't asking you to wear a burlap sack, but he is asking you to put on a garment of kindness and compassion and to serve him by serving others.

If your relationship with food is complicated by health issues or disordered eating, consider other ways you might fast. For example, you can refrain from watching television, using social media, or consuming caffeine. Remember that the heart behind your decision to fast is what matters most to God.

3. **Enter God's house.** Joel is not suggesting you enter your local church as a casual observer. He says, "Call a sacred assembly. Summon . . . all who live in the land to the house of the LORD your God, and cry out to the LORD" (Joel 1:14).

My father was a pastor, so as a kid I found myself sitting in church every time the doors were open. I wasn't the most attentive, and I mastered the art of napping upright in a pew. I would sit in the back of the church so my dad couldn't see my eyes were shut. From a distance, he thought I was nodding my head "amen" when I was actually nodding off. To pass the time in church I invented brain games. I created nicknames for members of the congregation. For example, there was a self-professed hippie who refused to wear shoes to church. I named him Dr. Scholls. We also had a worship leader who was painfully off-tune. My nickname for him was Earplugs. And one woman put her hair in the highest bun I'd ever seen. She was Bird's Nest.

At that time I didn't grasp the value of the house of God, but later in my life church participation became an opportunity, not an obligation. Church offers a place to learn God's Word, fellowship with others, and be encouraged. There's nothing sacred about brick and mortar, but it is enriching to come to a place that bears the name of Jesus and invites his presence.

Foundations Matter

Your heart is the foundation God builds upon. If you don't attend to cracks and character weaknesses, the flaws will grow over time and limit what God can build. What you accomplish for God starts with the condition of your heart. You can build a temporary foundation that may make a splash in the world, or you can build it right and make it last.

It was October 17, 1989. My friend Dave had scored two tickets to Game 3 of the World Series between the San Francisco Giants and the Oakland A's. We were seated in the nosebleeds—the upper deck, one row from the top of the stadium. At 5:04 p.m., Candlestick Park began to convulse from a magnitude 6.9 earthquake. It was the only time I've ever seen cement ripple like waves. From my seat, I could see a seam in the cement separate, the light towers bend, and the upper deck sway. Later we learned pieces from the upper deck fell, and the Bay Bridge and other freeways collapsed. Over 3,700 people suffered injuries, and 63 people died. The game was canceled, and fans were sent home. Because of the damage to infrastructure and buildings, it took us seven hours to drive thirty-five miles from San Francisco to the East Bay. That night, Dave, an architect, explained how the stadium's foundation had saved our lives and those of thousands of other fans. "There are two kinds of foundations—firm and faulty," he said. "If the foundation had been faulty and braces hadn't held, we wouldn't be here."

Living encouraged is directly tied to the stability of our foundation. Jesus tells us how to build a strong one:

> As for everyone who comes to me and hears my words and puts them into practice, I will show you what they are like. They are like a man building a house, who dug down deep and laid the foundation on rock. When a flood came, the torrent struck that house but could not shake it, because it was well built. (Luke 6:47–48)

To establish a firm foundation, Luke provides three words of instruction:

1. Come to Jesus (pray).
2. Hear his words (read his Word).
3. Put them into practice (obey his commandments).

I was driving my daughter Lauren to elementary school one day when she blurted, "Dad, is Jesus with us right now?" I replied, "Yes, Jesus is everywhere." She asked, "Is he sitting in that seat next to you?" I said, "Yes, he is." With a puzzled expression, she then asked, "If Jesus is here, shouldn't we be talking to him?" To her credit, Lauren understood that prayer isn't limited to church; it's honest and heartfelt conversation with the Lord. We can talk to him anytime we want because he's always listening. When you and I face disappointment and betrayal, we can come to Jesus. When we have financial setbacks and stress keeps us awake at night, we can tell Jesus how we feel.

One young man shared with me that he was having a challenging time. He said, "God just seems so far away. I feel like I'm hanging out on a limb all by myself." I thanked him for his transparency, then added, "God doesn't expect you to pretend everything is fine. The truth is the world is in crisis, and God wants you to turn to him rather than only retreating to video games, for example, to escape the madness. He wants you to be honest with him. Tell him how you're feeling. You don't need to censor or sanitize your prayers. It requires more faith to entrust your cares, fears, and disappointments to God than it does to try to hide them."

> Remember, authentic faith—not artificial faith—moves the heart of God.

Perhaps you can relate to how this young man felt. It's okay to say, "God, it's been a difficult few years. My happiness has been eroded by months of uncertainty and all the fear and conflict swirling around me. I'm weary, and I need your help." Remember, authentic faith—not artificial faith—moves the heart of God.

Good Company

Some relationships feel safe—you can take off your shoes, let your hair down, and lower your guard with that person. They help you push the reset button. You are mentally, emotionally, and physically free from harm or risk. Other relationships are "unsafe." The use of that word doesn't suggest the person poses a threat. It just means the relationship lacks familiarity or trust.

Prior to a formal awards banquet, I found myself cornered by a guest who unabashedly shared his opinions on every topic imaginable. I chose my words carefully and avoided eye contact. The conversation wasn't being recorded, but I knew everything I said would likely be repeated. My ears burned with his endless complaints and criticism. And, to make matters worse, he petitioned for my approval and agreement. I literally had to bite my tongue because I didn't want to create a scene. We were standing near a large punch bowl filled with a red beverage. As his scathing remarks intensified, I inched closer to the punch bowl. I wasn't thirsty—I was fighting the temptation to do "God's work" by dumping it on the man's head. As far as I was concerned, he needed to cool down. Fortunately, Doree tapped me on the shoulder before I did something I'd regret. This relationship wasn't a safe space because I couldn't trust him to use discretion or avoid gossip. Twenty minutes of listening to his rants raised my blood pressure. Some people are stress producers; they add to your worry and sap your happiness. Caring for yourself—and pushing reset—means limiting the amount of time and energy you invest in unsafe relationships.

You can also start investing in relationships with people who replenish you—people who encourage you and cause you to think in new and creative ways.

Jesus Rested

Rest can help you regain perspective and live encouraged. Have you ever thought of rest as an act of kindness? If you're someone who tends to overwork and undersleep, you're not alone. Our culture glamorizes seventy-hour workweeks, the daily grind, and being the colleague first to arrive at the office and the last to leave. But actually, if you are sleep-deprived, more rest may be what you need most to succeed. When I asked a billionaire to explain the secret to his financial success, he replied, "Leisure time." You might read that and think, *Well, of course he would say leisure time—he can afford it.* And you're not wrong. An abundance of free time is not realistic for most of us. But taking a Sabbath is both realistic and necessary.

Jesus advocated taking a Sabbath, because he knew a day of rest supports physical, emotional, and spiritual health. John Mark Comer, author of *The Ruthless Elimination of Hurry*, describes God's invitation for us to join him in the

> interplay of work and rest. And when we don't accept his invitation, we reap the consequences. Fatigue. Burnout. Anxiety. Depression. Busyness. Starved relationships. Worn-down immune systems. Low energy levels. Anger. Tension. Confusion. Emptiness. These are the signs of a life without rest. . . . You can skip the Sabbath—it's not sin. It's just stupid.[3]

Take another look at your calendar and ask yourself what steps you can take to be kind to yourself and find more rest. Rest is a spiritual act; it's not optional or a luxury. It's necessary. You don't have to go far to find the scientific evidence: the Mayo Clinic, Johns Hopkins Medicine, and the Centers for Disease Control, to name a few, agree that "insufficient sleep has been linked to the development and management of a number of chronic diseases and conditions."[4]

If I were to start Convoy of Hope today, I would do it much differently. I would expect less of me and more of God. I would rely less on my work ethic and more on the miraculous. At times, I approached the ministry as if it were an Iron Man competition, pushing myself to extremes when God wanted me to simply stretch my faith on my knees. It's easy to grow accustomed to the challenge—the daily grind—rather than the divine. We endure the frustrations that accompany self-sufficiency rather than rely on the work of the Holy Spirit.

Rest reenergizes us, but it is also a time to stop and hand God the microphone. We can wake up from a nap or good night's sleep with fresh ideas and a godly perspective. Sleep is not time wasted; it is an investment in tomorrow.

Prioritizing rest is easier said than done. It means guarding our calendar and managing how we respond to people and pressures in our day-to-day lives. The Cleveland Clinic published an article entitled "Why Downtime Is Essential for Brain Health," which suggests these practical steps:

1. **Schedule *actual* downtime.** Fun activities and scrolling social media do not count as downtime. "These activities all require processing information—and part of the reason we need more downtime is that we're doing way too much processing already," psychologist Dr. Scott Bea explains. Even spending a few minutes letting your mind wander or daydream supports mental health.

2. **Plan time to ponder things that cause you to worry.**
   You might call this intentional procrastination.
   There's nothing wrong with preserving mental energy until you need to make decisions.
3. **Take advantage of available tools.** Examples include
   using an app for guided prayer or meditation or listening to instrumental music.
4. **Tune in to your senses.** Listening to birds, for example, can help you "pay attention to your senses rather
   than your thoughts."[5]

Find Your "Fishing"

Escaping stress and remaining encouraged is an art, but too
often we resort to ineffective stress removers. For some people,
fishing is relaxing, therapeutic, and life-giving. But for me fishing has been bittersweet. I am quite possibly the worst fisher
on the planet. My escapades on water are fit for a TV sitcom.
I've fallen out of a paddleboat, been shot out of a speed boat,
embedded a fishing hook in my daughter's leg, smashed boats
into rocks, and lost a lot of expensive fishing tackle. And, to
make matters worse, I haven't had much luck catching fish. I
think Doree's family has unofficially banned me from fishing
trips. I was once invited to speak on a dinner cruise, and I was
tempted to cancel for fear the boat could capsize.

Don't get me wrong; I enjoy fishing. But for safety reasons,
I would prefer to head to a secluded beach with an umbrella,
sunscreen, and a spy novel. Each person's tastes are different,
so it makes sense that our paths to encouragement won't
look the same.

Living encouraged is seldom accomplished overnight. Most often it requires taking many small steps. Just making a little progress each day is beneficial—and will take you further than you may think. When I decided to shed some inches from my waist, I knew it would take time, and I wouldn't see immediate drastic progress. Nonetheless, I was impatient; I wanted to reunite with my former wardrobe as soon as possible. But I also wanted to be sure my choices were sustainable. So I began with an achievable goal: I eliminated desserts from my diet. No ice cream, no cake, no candy—no fun. But to my surprise, I quickly began to lose weight and found I had more energy.

Ask yourself, *What small steps can I take to be more encouraged?* Here are a few ideas as you create your own list:

1. Declutter your house by storing, donating, or throwing away unnecessary items.
2. Avoid watching television programs or movies that trigger negative thoughts or behavior.
3. Take a break from news programs or podcasts that feed into discouragement.
4. Set aside time each week for enjoyable exercise.
5. Limit your exposure to social media or take a break from it altogether for a week or month.
6. Join a small group Bible study and make attending church services part of your weekly schedule.
7. Meet with a Christian counselor or therapist who can support you as you pursue greater physical, emotional, mental, and spiritual health.
8. Plan a vacation or short getaway.

9. Take time for a hobby or do something you love that taps into your creativity.

10. Focus on the future rather than being stuck in the past. Let go of shame, resentment, and grief.

The Lord wants to accompany you on this journey to greater encouragement. A good place to start is to pray like David in Psalm 25:

> Direct me, [God], throughout my journey
> so I can experience your plans for my life.
> Reveal the life-paths that are pleasing to you. . . .
> Keep showing the humble your path
> and lead them into the best decision.
> Bring revelation-light that trains them in the truth. . . .
> Who are they that live in the holy fear of [God]?
> You will show them the right path to take.
>   (vv. 4, 9, 12 TPT)

7

LOST AND FOUND

When Jesus looked at Mary and saw her weeping at his feet, and all her friends who were with her grieving, he shuddered with emotion and was deeply moved with tenderness and compassion. . . . Then tears streamed down Jesus' face. Seeing Jesus weep caused many of the mourners to say, "Look how much he loved Lazarus."

John 11:33–36 TPT

Hal, I just found out I have COVID. You need to go get yourself checked out." That was the voice message left on my cell phone by my friend and Convoy of Hope board member David Cribbs. The previous day we had met for breakfast to discuss the construction of our new world distribution center. Exiting the restaurant, he'd given me a hug, saying, "Hal, I love you, man." He'd said that before, but this time seemed unusually heartfelt.

A few days later, David was admitted to the hospital. Two weeks went by with minor improvement. Then, early one morning, his son Mike called to notify me his father had passed.

David was an accomplished businessperson, widely loved and respected in his community. He was committed to God's work and helped countless people. I'd hoped he'd live forever. At his funeral, before a packed auditorium, I spoke about his kindness, integrity, and generosity. I shared how I had leaned heavily on his counsel and how we'd served together in the trenches of compassion ministry for two decades. And now, with his passing, I confessed I felt a huge void in my life.

David was one of six close friends who passed in fourteen months. Relationships I counted on unexpectedly vanished. I couldn't help but wonder who was next, and whether the virus would come calling for me as well. Part of grieving, says clinical psychologist and University of Arizona professor Mary-Frances O'Connor, is learning how to be in the world without a loved one. "The background is running all the time for people who are grieving," she says. "[They are always] thinking about new habits and how they interact now."[1]

COVID-19 affected members of Convoy of Hope's team and my family. It was difficult to understand the unpredictability. Some people became deathly ill; others had minor, cold-like symptoms. While the political debate raged over vaccines, masks, and effective treatments, I couldn't understand how some entirely dismissed the virus and its risks. My friends were dying, and, like many, I felt helpless. "The pandemic—and the political battles and economic devastation that have accompanied it—have inflicted unique forms of torment," says Holly Prigerson, codirector of the Cornell

Center for Research on End-of-Life Care.[2] She goes on to describe the aftermath as a "grief pandemic." In the midst of so much personal pain and community heartbreak, all I could do was pray and work to ensure the fleet of Convoy of Hope trucks filled with food and supplies kept rolling. So much changed in a short period of time, and I found myself experiencing cumulative grief, when you mourn multiple losses at the same time.[3]

Las Vegas businessperson Scott Howard also served on our board of directors until he succumbed to cancer. For years, Scott battled the disease and underwent multiple surgeries and chemotherapy. When he'd joined the board, he and I began to talk and pray together nearly every week. His faith and courage were an inspiration to many. Rather than complain about his declining health, he wanted to talk about helping the poor and suffering. I would ask, "Scott, how are you doing?" In response, he'd say, "I'm doing okay—I'm excited about all the things God has for us to do." Then one night, he called me from his hospital bed and asked me to pray. It was the last time I would hear his voice.

Another longtime friend and businessperson, Bob Clay, also contracted COVID-19. He served on the board of directors for a decade and was a trusted adviser on a wide range of topics. When doctors placed him in isolation, no one was permitted to see him. In the early days of Convoy of Hope, he and his wife, Rosa, had made generous donations to sustain the ministry. So, on numerous occasions, I introduced Bob as "one of the founders." Before his passing, his son Rob arranged for me to speak to him on a video call. Bob's speech was labored and his breathing strained, so I kept my comments brief: "Bob," I said, "thank you for making me

a member of your family. I love you. Thank you for investing in my life." Tears flowed down my face because I knew
there would be no more impromptu coffee shop meetings.
No more road trips. And no more "after work" phone calls.

The loss of my brother-in-law, Ron Waggoner, was equally
numbing. After retiring from the insurance industry, he and
his wife, Cheryl, moved to Missouri to help us expand the
work of Convoy of Hope. Day after day, he telephoned donors to thank them and pray with them. His faithfulness to
the mission was legendary. Then he was diagnosed with Alzheimer's. He'd been affable and athletic, and it was difficult
to watch him decline. At his funeral, I said, "Ron, if you're
listening, thank you for your friendship . . . and thanks for
being a friend to the poor."

When it came to close friends, my goal was to give them
more than they gave me. But with David, Scott, Bob, Ron,
and others, that was impossible. I received so much more
from their friendship, and Convoy of Hope benefited enor-
mously from their wisdom and generosity. We weren't friends
because we were in constant need of each other's encouragement. Rather, we were brothers on a mission to reach the
poor and suffering around the world. They stood by my side
when bank accounts were meager and the enemy was on the
war path. But, in a matter of months, a large part of that
support system disappeared.

Grieving Losses

Ajita Robinson, a grief and trauma expert, describes how "a
lot of people have a difficult time naming their losses because
our society is geared toward grief being limited to physical

loss, and it really negates the impact of symbolic losses that we encounter on a daily basis."[4]

Perhaps you're grieving such "other losses"—not just relational but financial or personal. You may be suffering from the loss of what you thought your life would look like. Maybe the stock market took an unexpected turn, a spouse was unfaithful, or chronic health issues have limited what you can do. Possibly the career path you thought you'd take isn't panning out like you'd hoped.

The loss you experience may not be a "big deal" to others, but it matters to you and matters to God. My family lost two beloved pets in a relatively short amount of time during the pandemic, and we all grieved that loss. We were comforted knowing God doesn't minimize our grief or tell us to "just get over it." Whatever you are grieving, those emotions are valid. Jesus understands what you're going through, and please understand you are permitted to grieve loss of any kind at any time.

In Job 1:10, Satan speaks to God regarding Job, God's servant. He says, "Have you not put a hedge around him and his household and everything he has? You have blessed the work of his hands, so that his flocks and herds are spread throughout the land." I felt like God had done that for me. He had erected a hedge of protection in the form of David, Scott, Bob, Ron, and others. But now it felt like the wall around me was missing huge sections and, as a result, I was more vulnerable to the attacks of the enemy.

Undeniably, the friendships I lost were irreplaceable. But I began asking God to help me rebuild my support system. I needed a circle of friends who would guard my back and hold me accountable. Everyone wants cheerleaders, but we also need friends who will tell us the truth. We need people in our lives who will encourage us to take care of ourselves and help us do the right thing.

Selecting an "inner circle" of friends—or personal board of directors—is much like a CEO assembling an executive team. Ideally, you want to include a variety of skill sets, personalities, and perspectives. But nothing is more important than friends who can discern God's will. Every one of us has imperfections and blind spots, so I wasn't looking for superheroes. It was more important for them to be humble and "live forgiven" than to appear to have it all together. I created a list of virtues (a profile) I wanted members of my inner circle to have. Granted, the expectations were significant, but I knew the stakes were high for my life and the work of Convoy of Hope. I saved the following list on my phone and also placed a hard copy in my briefcase:

> Everyone wants cheerleaders, but we also need friends who will tell us the truth.

Loyal. They give you the benefit of the doubt when others don't.

Prayerful. They take matters to prayer and seek God's direction.

Trustworthy. They are committed to doing the right thing.

Biblical. They filter decisions through the Word of God and base their behavior on biblical principles.

Confidential. They exercise good judgment in sharing information.

Resourceful. They are problem solvers.

Strategic. They can identify the proper steps toward achieving a stated goal.

Generous. They have a track record of giving without expecting anything in return.

Compassionate. They go beyond pity and respond to the needs of hurting people. They don't stand on the shoulders of the poor; they invite the poor to stand on theirs.

Kingdom minded. They see the kingdom of God as a composite of churches and people rather than one particular denomination or ministry.

Available. They are willing to invest time in significant friendships.

In a matter of months, God answered my prayers and encircled me with friends who possessed amazing qualities. Once again I was reminded that when we suffer loss, our God specializes in restoring and replenishing. We simply need to ask him to bring the right people into our lives at the right time. I still grieved the loss of my loved ones, but I no longer felt unprotected and vulnerable.

Healthy Gratitude

Jesus surrounded himself with twelve disciples to pursue the Great Commission. But he was interested in more than their man-hours and skill sets. He also valued their friendship. Too often relationships are underappreciated until they are gone. Perhaps subconsciously, we take them for granted. In most areas of our lives, lack of gratitude is the default setting, and it affects everything—how we feel, think, and act. "If you fail to carry around with you a heart of gratitude for the love you've been so freely given, it is easy for you not to love others as you should," says author and pastor Paul David Tripp.[5]

Gratitude is a powerful change agent. "A growing body of research is confirming that an ounce of gratitude is worth a pound of cure," according to UC Davis Health Medical Center.[6] Studies link higher levels of gratitude with better health—physically, mentally, and emotionally. A group at UC Berkeley notes that

> one study found that more grateful cardiac patients reported better sleep, less fatigue, and lower levels of cellular inflammation, and another found that heart failure patients who kept a gratitude journal for eight weeks were more grateful and had reduced signs of inflammation afterwards. Several studies have found that more grateful people experience less depression and are more resilient following traumatic events.[7]

Although gratitude may come more easily to some than others, it isn't a quality you either have or don't. If gratitude doesn't come naturally to you, you can improve with repetition.[8] It's likely you will notice a greater benefit over time, so don't be discouraged if you don't see changes right away.[9] Here are a few ideas for practicing gratitude:

- Write a gratitude letter (or send a text) to someone.
- Pray and thank God for things for which you are grateful.

- Start a gratitude list on your phone and challenge yourself to add something new each day.
- Place sticky notes on your refrigerator or write thank-you notes to Jesus on your mirror with a dry erase marker.
- Make it a practice to thank restaurant servers and other service providers—and mean it.
- Count the number of times you say thank you in a given day. (Hopefully your loved ones and coworkers are receiving a healthy portion of your gratitude.)

Forgiveness vs. Reconciliation

Losing a friend to COVID-19 or other fatal disease is tragic, but it's also agonizing to lose someone from your life due to personal conflict. The pain and resentment of losing a friend that way can linger for years. Often it takes an event or tragedy to bring closure and for both parties to realize that winning an argument at the expense of a friendship is too great a cost. Reconciliation is the ultimate goal, but that requires respect, fairness, forgiveness, compromise, accepting responsibility, and evidence of changed behavior. Usually, it comes down to someone saying, "I was wrong—forgive me."

Reconciliation requires forgiveness, but forgiveness does not require reconciliation. Forgiveness is a transaction between you and God. It means handing him your pain and letting him carry it; it's trusting him to be the author of justice. Ephesians 4:32 says, "Be kind and compassionate to one another, forgiving each other, just as in Christ God forgave you."

Forgiveness is unilateral. Even if the other person never repents or acknowledges the wrong they have done, we are commanded to forgive. Jesus said, "When you stand praying, if you hold anything against anyone, forgive them, so that your Father in heaven may forgive you your sins" (Mark 11:25). On the other hand, reconciliation is bilateral. It requires the offender to acknowledge their offense, repent, and show evidence of change.

Here are some principles to follow when you find yourself in conflict with a friend:

1. Avoid making a business disagreement a personal grievance.
2. Check your motives. Why is this important to you?
3. Be open to compromise.
4. Refrain from slander. Let God champion justice.
5. Be willing to apologize for your role in the conflict, even if it seems small to you.
6. Consider engaging a mediator to bring resolution.
7. Make honorable and honest decisions, regardless of the opinions of others.

When conflict arises, devote the matter to prayer. Trust God to provide healing and justice. It's not always easy to step back from painful situations and put God in charge. But it takes more faith to hold steady than it does to mount a counteroffensive. Exodus 14:14 says, "The LORD will fight for you; you need only to be still." *Be still*—that can feel like a very tall order when you've been wronged. Psalm 20:7 says, "Some find their strength in their weapons and wisdom, but my miracle-deliverance can never be won by men. Our boast is in Yahweh our God, who makes us strong and gives us victory!" (TPT). Keep praying that God performs a miracle and uses the disagreement to usher in a new level of understanding and respect.

Years ago, a friend who owned a business told me the story of an employee who resigned from his position to launch his own company. On his way out the door, he maligned coworkers, threw insults at his former employer, and pridefully stated in his exit interview that he knew how to do things much better but his supervisor wouldn't listen. He also made unfortunate statements on social media, announcing to the world that he was destined for "greater things." Regrettably, he burned bridges with his former employer and turned one-time advocates into adversaries.

> It's not always easy to step back from painful situations and put God in charge. But it takes more faith to hold steady than it does to mount a counteroffensive.

He moved to another state to start his business. But when he didn't experience the success he envisioned, he appealed to his former employer for another job. As you can imagine, the business owner refused to grant him an interview. Of course, his former employer could and did forgive him. But reconciliation wasn't possible because he never apologized to his coworkers or accepted responsibility for his behavior.

If you've lost a friend due to conflict, perhaps even a member of your inner circle, do what you can to bring healing and civility. Then trust God to do what only he can.

The Jury

In my twenties, I was selected to serve on the jury of a highly publicized court case in the San Francisco Bay Area. A local media personality had been shot and was now quadriplegic. Because of major news coverage, the judge placed a gag order on the trial and vowed to sequester the jury if there were any news leaks. At the end of each day, we were ushered out of the courtroom through a secure passage to avoid the mob of reporters and cameras.

When the victim was wheeled into the courtroom on a hospital bed, the jurors became like statues. We sat in stunned silence. None of us were prepared to hear her emotional testimony spoken through a ventilator. Some jurors brushed tears from their eyes as she told her tragic story.

The defendant was charged with attempted murder, despite the absence of the weapon or any eyewitnesses. As a result, the prosecuting attorney built his entire case on circumstantial evidence. In his closing statement, he spoke directly to the jurors. He said in order to acquit the defendant, we had to believe his girlfriend and best friend had given false testimony, he just happened to be on that highway when the shooting took place, the time stamp at the gas station was incorrect, his truck was hidden in a country barn for legitimate reasons, and another driver had randomly guessed the perpetrator's make of vehicle. To acquit, he said, the jury had to believe all this was a coincidence and the defendant had the worst luck on the planet. It took the jury five days to reach a verdict, but the defendant was convicted on all counts.

After that courtroom experience, I lost faith in coincidence. Our lives don't swing from side to side because of happenstance. Jesus didn't die on a cross, rise again, and then check out, leaving us at the mercy of random circumstances. I still don't know all the reasons my father was taken from us, but I do know God didn't allow the story to end on that day. He took all the broken pieces and the uncertainties and wrote a beautiful story. If I hadn't gone through the experience of poverty and generosity from others as a child, due to his death, would I have felt called to start Convoy of Hope? God took my father's mangled automobile and transformed it into a fleet of trucks that would deliver help and hope to millions of people.

Fortunately, God is still writing stories with beautiful endings. When the enemy sends hardship and tragedy our way, God takes the enemy's story and rewrites it for his glory. That's what he did for Joseph in the book of Genesis. Responding to his brothers' betrayal and the ensuing difficulties, Joseph says, "You intended to harm me, but God intended it for good to accomplish what is now being done, the saving of many lives" (Gen. 50:20).

When the lives of friends such as David Cribbs, Scott Howard, Bob Clay, and Ron Waggoner converged with Convoy of Hope, they didn't enter God's script by coincidence. It was destiny—the providence of God. Likewise, the partners who fuel Convoy of Hope today are part of that same compelling story.

The friends in my life and yours are not there by mistake. They deserve to be treasured. God brought you together to guard each other's backs, protect one another's hearts, and advance his kingdom. If that resonates with you, perhaps now is the perfect time to message someone and express how much you value their friendship.

8

YELLING "OUCH"

Then seizing him, they led him away and took him into the
house of the high priest. . . . The men who were guarding
Jesus began mocking and beating him.

Luke 22:54, 63

On occasion, we're all inclined to feel sorry for ourselves.
But when we throw a pity party, the enemy is the only
one celebrating. Perhaps we've been cheated, mistreated,
overlooked, or overbooked, and the world feels as cruel as
ever. Amid all the chaos and injustice, we begin to tell ourselves, *Woe is me*. We forget that millions around the world
are suffering with no hope in sight. Many have lost everything they owned and everyone they loved. That fact doesn't
invalidate how we feel, but it does put it into perspective.

After interviewing Aleks, a twenty-one-year-old Ukrainian refugee, I vowed I'd never complain again. He had been studying at a university in Mariupol, Ukraine, when Russia invaded the city. "There were airstrikes all day and night," he said, "and shelling and gunshots. Buildings were set on fire and people killed."

Aleks hid in a basement and later in an overcrowded shelter. Food was scarce, and they were forced to wait in long lines for a liter of water. At night, families huddled together to cry and pray, he said, as airstrikes relentlessly pummeled nearby buildings.

Then tanks rolled into the city, and the Russian soldiers commandeered the shelter. Families were driven to the streets and ordered to evacuate. Aleks was among the fortunate ones—he was able to stow away on a bus that transported him across the border into Russia. "As I left Mariupol," he said, "I looked back and all I could see was smoke and rubble."

Eventually Aleks escaped through Estonia and landed in Warsaw, Poland. When I asked if he would ever return to Mariupol, his face became like stone. "There is nothing to go back to," he said. "Everything has been taken from us."

I regretted asking the question. "I'm sorry," I said. "But please know a lot of people around the world want to help."

He nodded. "I know—and we will never forget that you came to Ukraine and brought us help when we needed it most."

Defending God

I don't pretend to understand why people are devastated by war, children die from malnutrition, women suffer neglect and abuse, and families are ravaged by natural disasters. For years, I attempted to defend God and explain catastrophes with a few canned slogans.

But I wasn't being honest with myself.

The truth is, I don't know why some people suffer and others don't. But I am basing my entire life on the fact God is good and he wants the best for everyone. When I get to heaven, there will be plenty of time to pose questions. (I'm sure he has some for me too.) In the meantime, like you, I want to stay busy working with Jesus to meet the physical and spiritual needs of as many people as possible. We can't allow unanswered questions to paralyze us. Doing something in partnership with God for those around us is always better than doing nothing.

Injustice and suffering may present a theological dilemma, but most non-Christians would prefer to hear us say "I don't know" than profess we have everything figured out. God doesn't expect us to memorize a slate of speculative answers to the mysteries of the universe. He'd prefer we speak honestly from the heart and let people know that following Jesus has changed our lives. We don't have to possess all the answers. We just need to be authentic, truthful, and sincere.

> We don't have to possess all the answers. We just need to be authentic, truthful, and sincere.

Speaking of honesty, nobody is accepting what we're advocating when we pretend we're happy about a job loss, a car breaking down, a knee acting up, a child getting suspended from school, a marital conflict, or a friend betraying our trust. When life hurts, it's okay to yell,

"Ouch!" God desires genuine emotion and conversation. You don't need to sound religious to win his approval: "Dear Master of the Universe, hear my humble cry. I beseech you, hallowed God, to deliver me from the clutches of the evil one. Thou art great. I sing 'Hallelujah' all day long. Have mercy on me." Instead, he relishes your heartfelt words and loves the sound of your unique voice: "Dear Jesus, I need your help. I've had a tough time lately. There's a lot I don't understand, but my faith in you will not be shaken. I know you thought of me when you hung on the cross. You came to my rescue when you rose from the grave. You've been with me through every challenge. My life and my future are squarely in your hands."

More than one third of the psalms are considered to be laments—honest confessions of hurt and complaints to God.[1] As king of Israel, David gave in to temptation and made huge mistakes, and yet God's heart was moved by his authenticity. David didn't mince words:

> God, give me mercy from your fountain of forgiveness!
> I know your abundant love is enough to wash away my
>   guilt.
> Because your compassion is so great,
> take away this shameful guilt of sin.
> Forgive the full extent of my rebellious ways,
> and erase this deep stain on my conscience.
> For I'm so ashamed.
> I feel such pain and anguish within me.
> I can't get away from the sting of my sin against you, Lord!
> Everything I did, I did right in front of you, for you saw
>   it all.
> Against you, and you above all, have I sinned.
>   (Ps. 51:1–4 TPT)

The Source of Hardship

Destiny is a complicated concept, especially when we suffer. We believe God has a plan for our lives, but it's difficult to see how a cancer diagnosis, a fractured relationship, or a financial setback can contribute to anything positive. Emotionally, hardship can become more confusing when a well-intentioned person says, "Everything happens for a reason." That expression is much different from the meaning of Romans 8:28: "And we know that in all things God works for the good of those who love him, who have been called according to his purpose." God is not the source of hardship. He does not initiate pain in our lives. Rather, he extricates us from it and eases the heartbreak. First Peter 5:8 reminds us that the enemy is the author of pain and suffering.

Following a church service, as I stepped off the stage, a woman requested special prayer. She said, "I'm not sure Jesus sees what I'm going through and how much I'm suffering. I don't know why this is happening to me." Immediately I sensed she was ashamed and embarrassed by her words. Before I could pray, she crumpled and began to cry. She had lost her job and been recently diagnosed with cancer. She felt abandoned and alone. I said, "Jesus sees everything you're going through, and he knows how you feel. He'll never take his eyes off you." After we talked and prayed for a few minutes, she was connected to a member of the pastoral staff so she could receive ongoing support.

If you are suffering from painful circumstances, Jesus wants you to know he hasn't gone anywhere. He's at your side and feels your pain. Hebrews 2:16–18 says,

It's obvious, of course, that he didn't go to all this trouble for angels. It was for people like us, children of Abraham. That's why he had to enter into every detail of human life. Then, when he came before God as high priest to get rid of the people's sins, he would have already experienced it all himself—all the pain, all the testing—and would be able to help where help was needed. (MSG)

Inevitable and Valuable

God never wastes hardship. Regrettably, sometimes we do. It's easier to retreat when the flames of life become uncomfortable, but sometimes God wants us to persevere. Hebrews 5:8 says, "Though [Jesus] was God's Son, he learned trusting-obedience by what he suffered, just as we do" (MSG). In his book *Walking with God through Pain and Suffering*, Tim Keller quotes Dan McCartney, who says, "Christ learned humanhood from his suffering (Heb. 5:8). [And therefore] we learn Christhood from our suffering." Keller adds, "Just as Jesus assumed human likeness through suffering (Heb. 2:18; 4:14–15), so we can grow into Christ's likeness through it, if we face it in faith and patience."[2]

Getting through hardship is a partnership between us and God. We aren't spectators who simply cheer for him from the sidelines. No, he invites us to do our part. For example, he may ask us to change our spending habits or increase our giving. He may nudge us to issue an apology, seek help from a counselor, or begin a Bible study. Or he may encourage us to play the role of peacemaker or walk away from a fight altogether. God's intervention in our hardship may begin with one act of obedience.

Our spiritual growth is stunted if we bolt toward comfort at the first sight of hardship. If we are led by self-preservation alone, the blessings God has for us may be delayed. James 1:3–4 says, "You know that the testing of your faith produces perseverance. Let perseverance finish its work so that you may be mature and complete, not lacking anything."

We don't have to like hardship—and we don't! I've never met anyone who says, "I'm thrilled to be practicing perseverance." But we can approach hardship with a different perspective. In 1 Thessalonians 3:4, Paul writes to followers of Jesus: "We warned you that troubles would soon come—and they did, as you well know" (NLT). Hardship is inevitable. That isn't the most encouraging thought, but we can count on God to intervene on our behalf. When challenges appear insurmountable, our God is greater. At times it may feel like the battle is being lost, but God

> At times it may feel like the battle is being lost, but God will help us press on and thrive in every test. When difficulties come, we can acknowledge they are both painful and valuable.

will help us press on and thrive in every test. When difficulties come, we can acknowledge they are both painful and valuable. They help shape us into powerful people of God.

It can feel impossible to see the benefits of obstacles and opposition, but through them we mature in so many ways.

1. **Reliance on God grows.** Proverbs 3:5–6 says, "Trust in the LORD with all your heart; do not depend on your own understanding. Seek his will in all you do, and he will show you which path to take" (NLT).

2. **Fear diminishes.** Second Timothy 1:7 says, "For God will never give you the spirit of fear, but the Holy Spirit . . . gives you mighty power, love, and self-control" (TPT).

3. **Hope increases.** Romans 15:13 says, "May the God of hope fill you with all joy and peace as you trust in him, so that you may overflow with hope by the power of the Holy Spirit."

4. **Vision expands.** Ephesians 3:20 says, "[He] is able to do immeasurably more than all we ask or imagine, according to his power that is at work within us."

5. **Strength multiplies.** Second Corinthians 12:10 says, "That is why, for Christ's sake, I delight in weaknesses, in insults, in hardships, in persecutions, in difficulties. For when I am weak, then I am strong."

Self-Awareness

As we partner with God to overcome hardship, we must remain self-aware. Hardship is not evidence of sin, but personal hardship can be a consequence of sin. When we reflect on our circumstances, we need to ask ourselves and God if there's anything we've done to contribute to our troubles. That was the case for an acquaintance who was unfaithful to his wife. Rather than confess his sin and seek forgiveness, he chose to live a lie. Meanwhile, on the surface, his businesses and investment portfolio appeared to be profitable. He lived in luxury and rubbed shoulders with community leaders. He gave generously to local schools, churches, and charities. He assumed God was looking the other way because his financial reserves were strong. But when his affair was revealed, the life he constructed crumbled. It had been built on a faulty foundation. He lost his marriage, and his businesses began to suffer. For years after that, he wrestled with deep regret and shame. He discovered that "success" can't atone for sin, nor hide it forever.

A pattern of sin is like swiping a credit card again and again. It gets more familiar each time and can make you feel like you aren't spending money. After all, it's just a flick of the wrist. But eventually the bill will come due. This man ultimately paid more than he ever expected. His decisions cost him nearly everything. Take a moment to ask yourself: *Am I making decisions that are shortsighted and lack wisdom? Are there areas of my life where I'm sinning, assuming the bill will never come due?*

Again, difficulty is not a definitive sign we are on the wrong path and outside the will of God. Sometimes he asks us to take more arduous routes to discover new truths and expand our faith.

God is at work 24/7, but we can become frustrated by "divine delays." How many times have you heard someone say, "I wish God would just hurry up and tell me what he wants"? Naturally we're ready to turn the page and move on. We don't always try to tell God what to do, but sometimes we tell him when to do it. We want God's calendar to reflect *our* timeline. Although it is sometimes difficult, we need to live according to God's schedule and let his purpose play out in our lives. If you have a health condition, pray for healing *and* perseverance. If someone has hurt you, pray for reconciliation *and* perseverance. If you have a financial need, pray for God's provision *and* perseverance. In other words, ask him to help you adopt his timeline.

I wish every hardship was short-lived or appeared to have a happy ending, but we don't live in a Pixar movie. Sometimes everything isn't wrapped with pretty bows, and we don't see God's outcomes. However, he promises to never desert us on the battlefield. He will be our protector. And, through every challenge, he will make us stronger. Please understand you may not *feel* stronger, because culture says strength is making it all look easy. But that's not always true. In an interview, actress Keira Knightley talks about this in the context of motherhood: "It's not strength if something's easy. It's strength when it's difficult and you come through it."[3]

With God, no battle will be wasted. He wants us battle-tested because the world needs us at our best.

Facing Injustice

When faced with great opposition and hardship, the prophet Habakkuk cried out to God:

> How long, LORD, must I call for help,
>   but you do not listen?
> Or cry out to you "Violence!"
>   but you do not save?
> Why do you make me look at injustice?
>   Why do you tolerate wrongdoing?
> Destruction and violence are before me;
>   there is strife, and conflict abounds.
> Therefore the law is paralyzed,
>   and justice never prevails.
> The wicked hem in the righteous,
>   so that justice is perverted. (Hab. 1:2–4)

In response, God provides Habakkuk with deeper understanding and a new perspective. He says, "Look at the nations and watch—and be utterly amazed. For I am going to do something in your days that you would not believe, even if you were told" (v. 5).

When we dissect the prophet's prayer, we can see he's asking the same three questions we ask when facing hardship:

1. God, where are you?
2. Why do I have to go through this?
3. When will it end?

Those are fair questions. But when hardship comes your way, you don't need to be reluctant to ask God for wisdom and the gift of faith to help you persevere. James 1:5 says, "If any of you lacks wisdom, you should ask God, who gives generously to all without finding fault, and it will be given to you." Few of us are naturally courageous in the face of adversity. If we have to depend on mental gymnastics or our ability to muster up enough courage, we're likely to fail. But that's where the gift of faith kicks in. We possess an assurance that Jesus is at work in every situation. We can rely entirely on his strength.

Medicine for the Soul

Just as there is a rhythm to hardship and miracles, we are meant to both laugh and cry. These are two parts of the same medicine to heal our mind, body, and soul. As Ecclesiastes 3:4 says, there is "a time to weep and a time to laugh."

Shedding tears because you are sad, mad, happy, or laughing uncontrollably is healthy; it releases cortisol and adrenaline, which help reduce stress and improve how we feel.[4] Holding in emotions related to hardship is unhealthy. "Studies have linked repressive coping with a less resilient immune system, cardiovascular disease, and hypertension, as well as with mental health conditions," according to social worker Leo Newhouse.[5]

One way to add laughter to your life is to creatively look for reasons to celebrate. When was the last time you threw a party—just because? You don't need holidays, birthdays, or sporting events to get together with friends. During the pandemic, we hosted family parties with our four daughters and two sons-in-law. Each gathering featured a unique theme: sports teams, Hollywood, the 1970s, the beatnik era, the color yellow, baby Yoda, and more. During those dark and heavy months, it gave us something to look forward to.

We don't have to chase adrenaline, but we should live with anticipation. That's where good planning comes in. Schedule vacations and days of refreshing throughout the year, and seldom cancel your plans. Make those days sacred. This is especially true for families. Our daughters knew I was committed to our family time. One year, during our Christmas family vacation, I received an invitation to attend a small gathering with the president of the United States in the Oval Office. I turned it down, because I wanted my children to know they were more important.

When hardship comes, having a fun activity to look forward to is therapeutic. That doesn't suggest you can't find relief from hardship right where you are. But sometimes healthy diversions—or counting down the days until a vacation or visit to an amusement park—can help you get through a rough stretch.

One Step at a Time

Following the 2011 EF5 tornado in Joplin, Missouri, Convoy of Hope Disaster Services sprang into action. Tractor-trailer loads of food, water, and emergency supplies descended on the wreckage within a few hours of the tornado, and our deliveries continued for months. More than 1,100 citizens were injured and 161 lost their lives.

On the one-year anniversary of the tragedy, the city held a ceremony to remember those who died and to honor the first responders. I was asked to deliver the keynote address to thousands of residents. That day I praised their hard work, unity, and courage.

In a time of great hardship, the citizens of Joplin sent the nation a message: hard work speaks louder than harsh words, and finding solutions is more important than affixing blame. They showed that in times of crisis, we can either focus our attention on a common vision or allow ourselves to be ensnared by division. They chose the former, and also chose to not be paralyzed by the size of the task ahead. Instead, they pressed on with determination and purpose. As a result, the city of Joplin was rebuilt and today is better than before.

Hardship is a defining moment for everyone. How we respond to tests and trials matters.

When staring opposition in the face, we can choose to retreat or, with God's help, we can roll up our sleeves and work to restore what was lost. That is the promise of 1 Peter 5:10: "And the God of all grace, who called you to his eternal glory in Christ, after you have suffered a little while, will himself restore you and make you strong, firm and steadfast."

9

NEXT QUESTION

He pulled away from them about a stone's throw, knelt down,
and prayed, "Father, remove this cup from me. But please,
not what I want. What do you want?"

Luke 22:41–42 MSG

As I stepped off the stage, a woman barreled toward me
from the rear of the auditorium. I wasn't sure if she was
planning to hug me or hit me, so I braced myself for a collision. Fortunately, she smiled and extended her arms for an
embrace. Then she pressed two $1 bills into my hand and
said, "God is asking me to give you this money to feed a
hungry child." As she walked away, the pastor leaned over
and whispered, "Hal, that woman is homeless. We're helping
her get off the streets, but she probably gave all she had."

Traveling home from that church service, I replayed the woman's words in my mind and pondered the significance of her offering. I sensed her gift mirrored the level of her gratitude. She owed God everything, so she gave him everything. That day, I was inspired and challenged by her act of obedience. But I was also struck by her words: "God is asking me to give you this." She believed she was honoring a request from the Lord.

We experience greater happiness and fulfillment when we ask God and ourselves the right questions. The homeless woman asked, "What does God want me to give?" Because she asked the right question, she received God's answer. She could have asked, "What can I give that I won't miss?" But that would have relegated her donation to a mathematical equation rather than an act of obedience. Generosity begins with asking God what he wants.

> We experience greater happiness and fulfillment when we ask God and ourselves the right questions.

God's instructions to care for the impoverished are threaded throughout Scripture. Isaiah 58:10–11 says, "Feed the hungry, and help those in trouble. Then . . . the LORD will guide you continually, giving you water when you are dry and restoring your strength" (NLT). And Luke 14:13–14 says, "But when you give a banquet, invite the poor, the crippled, the lame, the blind, and you will be blessed. Although they cannot repay you, you will be repaid at the resurrection of the righteous."

God, however, does not want us to extend a helping hand to the poor and suffering because we feel guilty for the blessings we enjoy. He does not ask us to take a vow of poverty;

he asks us to make a commitment to generosity. He doesn't ask us to trade places with the poor or to empty our bank account and give every penny away. He asks us to simply live with radical gratitude and obedience for all he has done for us.

Conversely, the enemy wants us to feel guilty for having so much and not doing enough for God in return. Here's a news flash: God doesn't *need* what we have to offer. He already has what he needs. He's extending an opportunity for us to partner with him to deliver beauty, healing, and kindness to the world. It's an opportunity—not an obligation.

On the cross, Jesus liberated us from the handcuffs of guilt and shame. The enemy wants us to believe we're still bound. But God is not a judge doling out punishment for every missed opportunity. He's our heavenly Father who forgives . . . and gives his children another chance to get it right. The Lord sums up his true expectations in Matthew 22, when Jesus says, "'Love the Lord your God with all your heart and with all your soul and with all your mind.' This is the first and greatest commandment. And the second is like it: 'Love your neighbor as yourself'" (vv. 37–39). We don't need to complicate our faith. We need to walk closely with Jesus and ask him to point out people who need our help along the way.

God's love and acceptance are not earned; they are freely given. His love is not allocated based on how much we give or how many people we help. He wants us to live with such gratitude that we ask the right question, like the homeless woman: "God, what do you want me to do?"

In Luke 10:30–37, a man's life was nearly lost because a priest and Levite asked the wrong question. Rather than rescue someone who had been attacked by robbers and left to die, they crossed to the other side of the road. They didn't stop because they asked, "What will happen to *me* if I help this person?" Their safety and comfort were more important than a human life. A Samaritan, however, took the time to bandage the man's wounds and take him to an inn for additional care. He even paid the bill. The Samaritan asked the right question. He asked, "What will happen to this person if I don't help him?" Doing the right thing begins with asking Christ-honoring questions.

Everywhere Jesus went, he encountered hurting people. He was willing to stop for anyone, and he simply did what his Father asked him to do. He expects the same attitude from us. In a world where we're surrounded by hurting people, Jesus isn't asking us to meet everyone's needs, because we can't. But we can, like the Good Samaritan, stop long enough to see the needs around us and ask the right question: "Father, do you want to demonstrate your love and compassion to someone through me?"

Checkups Needed

Each month, I've found it beneficial to ask God (and myself) a series of questions. You might call it a "wellness check" of sorts. You may choose to construct your own list, but the following eight questions have helped monitor my spiritual, emotional, and physical health:

1. Am I taking care of myself?

If you systematically ask the right questions, you are more likely to make corrections before they become larger problems. For example, some years ago I found myself losing sleep because I was contemplating heavy issues at night. Perhaps it was my journalism training, but my desire to know was interrupting my sleep. Some nights, as I lay awake after midnight, I'd grab my phone and begin making notes on everything from theology to Convoy of Hope business to famine in Africa. Obviously intermittent sleep wasn't helping me find peace. So, I asked myself and God what steps I needed to take to prepare for a good night's rest. Below are some of the changes I incorporated into my routine (with varying degrees of success):

- Discipline myself not to entertain weighty topics after 8:00 p.m.
- Reduce time spent on email and my phone after dinner.
- Review my calendar for the next day *before* dinner.
- Follow guidelines for healthier nighttime snacks and regular exercise.
- Retire to bed at the same time as my wife.
- Before turning out the lights, pray for rest, wisdom, and the gift of faith.
- Read a promise from God's Word each night and specifically surrender each major concern to him.
- Redeem time in the car, on airplanes, and in other similar settings to explore solutions to significant issues.

2. What is my spiritual temperature?

When the pace of life is too fast, we can run through spiritual stop signs. We speed ahead without knowing what God thinks, because our prayer life, Bible reading, and church attendance may have waned. If your spiritual temperature is tepid, you can change that by repenting of sin and confessing your need to the Lord. First John 1:9 says, "But if we confess our sins to him, he is faithful and just to forgive us our sins and to cleanse us from all wickedness" (NLT). You can rebound quickly if you are willing to stop and have an honest conversation with God. Psalm 37:7 says, "Be still before the LORD and wait patiently for him."

3. What am I holding on to?

After dislocating my finger by swinging a golf club, I figured it was time to take a few golf lessons. At first, the instructor said he would transform my swing in "five easy lessons." After the fifth lesson, he said, "I think it will take five more." He had either overestimated my ability or inflated his tutoring skills. During one lesson, the instructor told me to loosen my stranglehold on the club. When I did, to my surprise the ball went straighter and farther.

Sometimes we hold on to our plans, aspirations, and possessions so tightly that we hinder what God wants to accomplish in our lives. He knows what will fulfill us better than we do, so his plan may (and probably will) look different from ours. Without realizing it, what we hold on to may be the very thing that is holding us back spiritually. Ask the Lord if there's anything in your life that needs to be released, such as a dream job, prized automobile, dating relationship, or more.

4. Am I happy and content?

Discontentment is a challenge everyone faces at one time or another. Happiness and contentment aren't necessarily the same, but they are frequently interlocked. Perhaps you aren't finding fulfillment in your job or are having a hard time making ends meet. There is a myriad of reasons for discontentment. You don't need to feel guilty for having those emotions. But, through prayer, you can learn to be content with where God wants you to be and what he wants you to have. In Philippians 4:11–12, Paul says, "I have learned to be content whatever the circumstances. I know what it is to be in need, and I know what it is to have plenty. I have learned the secret of being content in any and every situation, whether well fed or hungry, whether living in plenty or in want."

Happiness and contentment come when we pursue God's timing—which frequently requires waiting. Too often, we rush into a decision or take action when God's perfect plan is to delay. Waiting for God to work or respond reflects our trust in him. In many situations, it requires more faith to exercise restraint than it does to launch out on our own.

5. How am I defining success?

How we answer this question is more revealing than we may think. When we define success as "obedience to God," we *are* successful. When we measure success only by finances, awards, accolades, or notoriety—we aren't.

Have you ever tried to use your arms to measure the width of a painting you're hanging on a wall? You put your hands on either side of the artwork, and then try not to move them as you walk across the room, doing your best not to distort the "measurement." Chances are the result isn't perfect because you weren't using the right measuring tool. That's the case for many people. We attempt to evaluate our level of success with the wrong rubric, so the results are unreliable. In God's eyes, we are successful, but often we don't think we are. Unfortunately, our brains have a negativity bias, meaning we "have a propensity to give more weight to things that go wrong than to things that go right—so much so, that just one negative event can hijack our minds in ways that can be detrimental to our work, relationships, health, and happiness."[1] So, the next time you become fixated on a negative thought, feeling, or belief about yourself or others, consider that your mind may be fooling you into thinking it comprehends more of the picture than it really does.[2]

6. Am I leading with kindness?

In an open forum at a university, a student asked me, "Since founding Convoy of Hope, how have you changed?" I replied, "Hopefully I'm not as judgmental and am more accepting of people, regardless of where they are. That's what Jesus did." I'm convinced people want to see that we value and accept them before they'll listen to what we have to say. When we lead with judgment or condemnation, we often forfeit the opportunity to share and demonstrate the love of Jesus. Why would anyone believe "Jesus is love" if we have a malicious spirit? Proverbs 18:16 says a gift opens the door for the giver. When we lead with kindness, it surprises, and it often redefines Christianity for those who are skeptical of our faith.

It's important to go beyond corporate compassion and practice personal kindness. Supporting a compassionate church or charity is good, but that's no substitute for personally helping people in need of a friend. Many years ago, I had the privilege of interviewing Mother Teresa in Kolkata, India, at her Kalighat Home for the Dying Destitutes. During our conversation, she asked, "Young man, what are you doing to help the poor and suffering?" I quickly determined it was not a good idea to lie to Mother Teresa, so I told her the truth. I said, "I'm really not doing much of anything." She replied, "Everyone can do something—just do the next kind thing God puts in front of you."

As people who are called to reflect the compassion and kindness of Jesus, we are concerned about the whole person. We emulate him by meeting physical and spiritual needs. In addition, we demonstrate kindness and concern by raising our voices and using our resources to combat racism, sex trafficking, homelessness, drug abuse, domestic violence, suicide, and more. We lead with kindness when we express interest in upgrading foster care and adoption programs, welfare systems, and prison reform, for example. Every human life has equal value, and delivering help and hope to people in the name of Jesus is our mission. Like Jesus, we respond to the needs of all people, regardless of their plight or political leanings.

7. What am I worried about?

Sometimes it's difficult to distinguish between worry and a spiritual burden. Both can interrupt sleep, change eating patterns, raise blood pressure, and much more. Worry is often fear-based; spiritual burdens are faith-based. Worry may not necessarily lead to prayer. Spiritual burdens almost always do. Worry is a weapon of the enemy. Spiritual burdens are a blessing from God. Philippians 4:6 says, "Don't worry about anything; instead, pray about everything. Tell God what you need, and thank him for all he has done" (NLT).

Spiritual burdens are often born out of righteous anger. Perhaps we're troubled by the nation's moral decay, the political divide, or the plight of the poor. In reaction to what he witnessed, Jesus became indignant on several occasions. Mark 1:40–42 says,

> A man with leprosy came to him and begged him on his knees, "If you are willing, you can make me clean." Jesus was indignant. He reached out his hand and touched the man. "I am willing," he said. "Be clean!" Immediately the leprosy left him and he was cleansed.

Note that Jesus was not angry at the man; he was indignant at the enemy for wreaking havoc on the man's life. Matthew 21:12–14 says,

> Jesus entered the temple courts and drove out all who were buying and selling there. He overturned the tables of the money changers and the benches of those selling doves. "It is written," he said to them, "'My house will be called a house of prayer,' but you are making it 'a den of robbers.'" The blind and the lame came to him at the temple, and he healed them.

On both occasions, Jesus follows a display of righteous anger with an act of compassion. He heals the leper, the blind, and the lame. Too often our outrage is followed only by more outrage and then destructive action.

Jesus is the greatest protester the world has ever known. He came to earth to redeem but also to protest the status quo. He denounced sin, poverty, oppression, racism, legalism, and more. Through word and deed, he peacefully and profoundly said, "Enough is enough—this is unacceptable." If we follow Jesus's example, there is a time and a place for righteous anger. (When we hear that sixteen thousand children die each day from hunger and water-related causes, we should have moral indignation.) But, like Jesus, we need the kind of anger that leads to prayer, compassion, and constructive action.

There *are* times to lift our voices for justice and declare the Word of the Lord, but we stake our future on the promise of 2 Chronicles 7:14: "If my people, who are called by my name, will humble themselves and pray and seek my face and turn from their wicked ways, then I will hear from heaven, and I will forgive their sin and will heal their land."

8. Am I too comfortable?

After interviewing Mother Teresa, I returned to the United States and began praying God would change my priorities and help me find new purpose. I was weary of living for myself and being isolated from a hurting world. I was growing spiritually weaker and, at the same time, more religious. For years, I confused isolation from non-Christians with purity and holiness. But Jesus never intended for us to hide behind the walls of our homes and churches. Instead, he calls us to look beyond people's exteriors and see the potential of their hearts. It doesn't matter if they're rich or poor, living in sin or not—they have a right to hear that Jesus loves them. To connect with this culture, we must be willing to go beyond words and get our hands dirty. We have to show people they matter to us and are valued by God. We need to go beyond pity to action. And, when we befriend those who are in need and unloved, we find personal peace and contentment. Because, at that moment, we're where Jesus would be and doing what he would do.

Sometimes, Jesus prods us to break out of our bubble and get uncomfortable. I know that sounds counterintuitive, especially when there's already an abundance of chaos in one's life. But when we're uncomfortable, we tend to become more reliant on God and know his presence. That's what happened to me. One day, I felt compelled to do something quite unusual—to travel to eight cities and walk the streets of each for three days and nights. I went to Miami, Atlanta, Chicago, Washington, DC, New York City, Detroit, Los Angeles, and Seattle. Along with friends, after midnight I interviewed drug addicts, gang members, prostitutes, runaways, and those experiencing homelessness. And in each city, I also rode with the police on their night shift. I visited crack houses, seedy bars, and jail cells and was involved in high-speed pursuits and chases on foot. I saw the underbelly of America up close and personal.

God used those experiences to break my heart and to open my eyes. For the first time, I began to see hurting and broken people as God's precious children. They weren't an inconvenience. They weren't a nuisance. They were God-given opportunities to demonstrate the love of Jesus. God had to do a work in my heart before he could do a work through my hands. It was on the heels of visiting these cities that we loaded up the first truck with groceries and began distributing them to working-poor families. That was the start of Convoy of Hope.

You don't need to walk city streets after midnight to get uncomfortable. (Also, without adequate security and training, this would probably be inadvisable and unnecessary.)

However, God may be asking you to step out of your comfort zone and do something impactful. Maybe it's taking a weeklong mission trip or volunteering to serve at an outreach event with your church—the menu of opportunities for service and reconnaissance is endless. Invite God to show you where he wants you to go or what he wants you to do. He's likely to give you a brand-new perspective.

After visiting those cities and rubbing shoulders with so many hurting people, my personal challenges and questions didn't seem so worrisome anymore. Like the homeless woman who gave a two-dollar offering, I was also exceedingly more grateful for all

> God had to do a work in my heart before he could do a work through my hands.

God's blessings. Rather than always asking him to do for me, I found myself asking, "God, what can I do for you?" That was the question that launched Convoy of Hope. And asking that question can change the trajectory of your life too.

10

CHANGING LANES

"Send the people away so that they can go to the surrounding
countryside and villages and buy themselves something to
eat." But [Jesus] answered, "You give them something to eat."

Mark 6:36–37

I learned a long time ago it's more fun to win than lose. In
sports, I've played for my share of losing teams. In fact,
I'm convinced I played for the worst church softball team ever
assembled. Over the course of two seasons, we didn't win a
game. It was so embarrassing the pastor of our church suggested we take the church's name off our jerseys. Half of our
team had never played organized softball or baseball—and
it showed. During one game, our eldest player was rambling
from first base to second and his hat blew off into center field.
With the ball still in play, he decided to bypass second base

and chase his hat into the outfield. The other team tossed the ball to the center fielder, who tagged him out.

Another game, our pitcher arrived inebriated. He walked the first four batters he faced. A few innings later, he was on the basepath and rounded third, heading for home plate. He lowered his shoulder and collided with the other team's catcher, knocking him out cold. Benches were emptied, punches were thrown, players were ejected, and our pitcher was suspended from the league. The brawl in the church league was the talk of the town for weeks. From that day on, we were known as the fighting church, which wasn't exactly helpful for attracting visitors.

A few of us were tired of losing, but all we did was complain without putting in the work to improve. But when the following season rolled around, we decided to pivot—to take a different approach. We assembled a new lineup of players and began holding mandatory practices. That year, we went from last place to first in the league. We went from being called the fighting church to being known as the winning church. And church attendance increased that year too.

Sometimes we struggle because we don't lay our challenges before the Lord and ask him to reveal new strategies. We tell ourselves it's easier to persist in chaos than go to the trouble of changing directions. When facing obstacles and delays, it's a perfect time to pray, "God, is there a better way?"

Timely Pivots

Many companies and organizations have famously started with one product or service and then pivoted to something different that skyrocketed them to success. The *Harvard Business Review* tells us, "Cornelius Vanderbilt switched from steamships to railroads, William Wrigley from baking powder to gum. Twitter launched as a podcast directory, Yelp began as an automated email service, and YouTube was once a dating site."[1]

Change can appear clear, compelling, and risk free in hindsight. But at the precipice—the edge of the cliff—it's not. The height makes our knees shake and distorts our vision, and the litany of what-ifs makes it impossible to focus. That's what big or small changes can feel like. The soundtrack of doubt plays on repeat in our heads.

What if I make a mistake?

What if I make the wrong decision?

What if I'm just not good enough?

As Convoy of Hope's workforce and volunteer base grew exponentially, it was apparent we needed to consider a new facility for US operations. Since its inception twenty-seven years earlier, Convoy had never constructed its own facility. We had maximized the space we had, with team members sharing offices and cubicles. But that wasn't cutting it any longer. The Missouri-based team was working from four facilities, and communication and coordination between departments was increasingly difficult. We ran the risk of teams becoming siloed and our efficiency lagging behind opportunity. It was clear we needed a new distribution center, global headquarters, and training center big enough to meet our needs. The team of employees and board of directors began to pray for open doors and God's direction.

One afternoon I asked board member David Cribbs a foreshadowing question: "David, what's the dream selling price for our current facility? What would we need to receive to confirm God wants us to relocate?" While he pondered my question, I went to a white board to write the number. He announced, "The number is $15 million. If God gives us that, we'll know he wants us to move." I said, "Okay, let's begin praying for $15 million." And I wrote it down.

Some weeks later, we received an offer for $15 million.

God answered one prayer; now we needed to know where he was taking us. Along with David Cribbs, chief of staff Keith Boucher, and chief business officer Kregg Hood, we began to explore dozens of land and building opportunities.

After months of searching, we purchased 127 acres through the generosity of five donors. Because of its topography and freeway visibility, it felt like this was our "promised land." But we immediately experienced unexpected and costly infrastructure issues. Eventually the board and executive team sensed God was closing that door, so, with the donors' permission, we placed the property back on the market and reinitiated our search.

When a prime piece of property at the entrance to the city became available, we agreed it had everything we hoped for: freeway access, infrastructure, and visibility. I told myself, *This must be the place God has in mind.* There was only one obstacle: the negotiated price was far above market value. Nevertheless, after due diligence, we presented a proposal to the board of directors for consideration. I said, "I know this is a lot of money, but Convoy of Hope will be the first sign people see when they enter the city. Thousands of cars will pass by every day. I believe this is God's will." After extended discussion, the board voted to move forward with the purchase. "This will be the future home of Convoy of Hope," we said—or at least that's what we thought.

A few months passed, and the price tag for developing the property continued to climb. I began to pray, "Lord, if I missed it—if this is not your will—please let us know before we consummate the purchase." One morning, I awoke with an uneasiness in my stomach. I knew we were racing ahead of God. This land was *our* solution—not his. The resources required to purchase and develop the land could temporarily affect our mission. That was unacceptable. As an organization, we had made a commitment not to do anything that would detract from our calling to serve communities, come alongside churches, feed children, empower women and farmers, respond to disasters, and more.

The next day, I had breakfast with David. I said, "David, I've already shared this with the leadership team, but I want you to hear it from me. We feel we need to walk away from the property. God has something else for Convoy." David nodded and said, "I feel the same way."

Six weeks later, in a board of directors meeting, I confessed that I had missed it. I said, "This feels like egg on my face, but doing God's will is all that matters. We believe God has another property for Convoy of Hope. This isn't the right site." David, Keith, and Kregg echoed those sentiments, and that day the board voted unanimously to go back to the drawing board a second time.

After that board meeting, disappointment, regret, and fatigue accumulated into a cloud of confusion. The board, leadership team, and others had invested countless hours in trying to make two different properties work, and now we were starting over. I felt like I had let everyone down by misunderstanding God's plan.

One night, as I was praying for a solution, I grabbed an iPad. I said, "God, all I want is your will. Please forgive me for coming to you with *my* plan. Show us where you want us to be." It was time for God to cast a deciding vote. I believed he had vetoed our plan because he had something better. I opened the iPad to Google Maps and asked the Lord to reveal the location. My eyes fell upon some vacant property off the freeway, in a part of the city I hadn't considered. The following morning, I met with Keith and Kregg and pointed out the property on a map. Kregg confirmed this was the same property that Tom Rankin, a friend and local developer, had proposed we investigate.

We met David at the property and surveyed the acreage from his ATV. Somehow this property felt different from all the others we had explored. Almost immediately, we sensed God's favor. The price was 25 percent of the previous property, with four times the acreage. In addition, it had excellent freeway access and infrastructure. With the board's approval, we closed on the purchase of the land in a matter of weeks.

In the months that followed, God confirmed in a number of ways that we were in his will. Friends, foundations, businesses, churches, and Convoy team members joined together to pledge $61 million to complete the new global headquarters and training center, which was named after longtime partners and friends Rick and Jan Britton and their family. Meanwhile, the mission of Convoy of Hope did not suffer. More children, mothers, farmers, disaster survivors, churches, and communities were being served than ever before.

When making major decisions now, I often reflect on how we almost missed out on God's plan. His location was far superior, and precious resources were saved. I was so grateful Convoy of Hope's leadership was willing to pivot—to retrace our steps and consider a different solution. Too often we settle for *okay*, *average*, or *easy* when God has something better planned. Sometimes we're so invested in one course that we're afraid to lose time, distance, and resources. But that's a small price to pay for God's perfect will. Proverbs 16:9 says, "We can make our plans, but the LORD determines our steps" (NLT).

Road Signs

God's visions and plans are often revealed to us in stages. While most of us would prefer to ride a high-speed elevator to the top floor, God, in his wisdom, knows it's sometimes in our best interest to climb the stairs to a vision—one step at a time. Vision is often incremental. He seldom reveals the complete roadmap or the final destination. Instead, he wants us to fix our eyes on him and rely on the Holy Spirit to guide our steps. Not knowing his entire plan can create a sense of uncertainty. Most of us don't like the unknown. An article by BBC writer David Robson summarized numerous studies that showed how "any element of unpredictability significantly increases people's discomfort." Our stress rises when something is possible but not guaranteed.[2] In other words, "play it by ear" and "up in the air" are not phrases we particularly enjoy. But we have been called to "walk by faith, not by sight" (2 Cor. 5:7 ESV).

The path God has for you includes lessons to learn and obstacles to navigate along the way. Without taking the journey, the destination will never be reached. God took Nehemiah on a journey to rebuild the wall of Jerusalem. The task was completed because Nehemiah sought and followed God's counsel. Examining the path to a fulfilled vision provides guidance for us today.

1. **Nehemiah felt a burden.** He was moved to tears and felt deep sorrow because the wall of Jerusalem had been breached and its gates set on fire. He mourned, fasted, and prayed for days before the vision came into focus (Neh. 2:1–4).

   A young pastor confided in me that he was having difficulty establishing a fresh vision for his church. "Do you have any advice?" he asked. "Yes," I said, "wake up each morning and pray for a God-sized burden for your community. God's vision begins with tears."

2. **Nehemiah had a plan.** He went beyond mourning to developing a strategy. Nehemiah was the king's cup-bearer. His job required attention to detail, so in this case God chose a planner to bring his vision to fruition (vv. 4–8). Part of planning is considering who will travel with you, so Nehemiah found the right partners. He couldn't rebuild the wall by himself, so he delegated tasks to those who possessed the right skills (chapter 3). He didn't exploit people; he created opportunities for them to tap into their God-given abilities to accomplish a God-given vision.

3. **Nehemiah persevered.** He prayed, planned, and part-nered. When the task became arduous and he was losing momentum, Nehemiah prayed for strength

and perseverance. Even though at times he wanted to throw in the towel, he knew he couldn't fail God or his people. He found the will to keep going and inspired his people to finish the task (chapter 4).

Persevering with Purpose

Years ago, when we were young parents and short on resources, Doree and I decided to drive twenty-five hours straight to her parents' home in Arizona. That would reduce our hotel and food costs. While the girls were preoccupied watching movies in the back of the van, Doree and I alternated driving. It was after midnight when she took the wheel, so we stopped at a convenience store to grab her some coffee.

I asked, "Have you ever tried Red Bull to keep awake?"

"Red Bull—what's that?" she replied. "What's it taste like?"

"It's some kind of power drink," I said. "I've never tried it, but I hear it works."

Minutes later, I watched her drink an entire can of Red Bull. "It's not bad," she said.

An hour passed. I fell asleep, and I awoke with a question: "Doree, are you wide awake—how are you doing?"

With more energy than I'd seen on her face in days, she blurted, "I'm grrrrrreat!" With the Red Bull working better than I expected, naturally I went back to sleep.

But by the time we arrived at our destination, we were both nearly comatose. (We should have bought a six-pack of Red Bull.) The circles under our eyes were the size of inner tubes. We had persevered and saved money, but we both came to the same conclusion: *we will never do this again.* From that marathon, we learned an important lesson: make sure you're persevering for the right things.

Like Nehemiah, continuing on your life's journey will require perseverance, and there may be seasons when you don't see the fruit of your labor. The successes and "wins" aren't visible yet. But that doesn't mean you aren't on your way. An article in the *Harvard Business Review* about our fear of the unknown provides research showing "most successful breakthroughs are produced by a series of small steps, not giant bet-the-farm efforts. Starting modestly can be more effective and less anxiety-provoking than trying to do everything at once."[3]

Some days will feel like nothing can go right: you have a pimple on your nose, you suffer from food poisoning, your future spouse calls off your wedding, your credit card bill is overdue, and your car runs out of gas. Yes, that would qualify as a rough day. But when circumstances are difficult and doubt creeps in, we need to remind ourselves we're not on this journey alone. Regardless of the terrain or the obstacles, each person has a God-given purpose. At one time or another, perseverance will be required to fulfill that purpose. No one escapes the need for perseverance—no one.

Remember, Jesus knows how you feel. In the face of physical pain, criticism, strife, weariness, obligations, human need, death, and more, he persevered. He endured so his purpose could be fulfilled. Hebrews 12:1–2 says, "Let us run with perseverance the race marked out for us, fixing our eyes on Jesus, the pioneer and perfecter of faith. For the joy set before him he endured the cross, scorning its shame, and sat down at the right hand of the throne of God."

Vision and Opposition

When a vision is from God, it invites opposition and doubt. But God doesn't call us to tasks we can't complete. He calls us to tasks we can't complete without *him*. We must learn to discern and trust the voice of God and ignore the voices of fear that attempt to dissuade, discourage, and deceive.

> God doesn't call us to tasks we can't complete. He calls us to tasks we can't complete without *him*.

Often, God confirms his vision or task by enlarging our burden. Nehemiah, for example, was so concerned about the state of Jerusalem that he wept. His tears reflected a heart that had been prepared for a God-given task. Today God is looking for prayerful and tearful servants whose hearts are breaking for the lost and suffering. He's looking for men and women who see the spiritual rubble yet refuse to throw up their hands in defeat. Instead, they raise their hands to God and say, "Lord, enlarge my burden and give me a vision to help people rebuild their lives."

I'm frequently asked, "How did you get the vision for Convoy of Hope?" My standard response is, "It was God's idea—his plan—we simply raised our hands and said we'd try." We don't own or create vision; we receive and manage God's vision. That's important to remember, as it's easy to make the mistake of assuming credit for what he has accomplished or feeling solely responsible when dreams don't go as planned.

If we are fulfilling a vision assigned by God, it's big enough—regardless of what other people might say or think. We tend to equate vision with size. We always hear about "huge vision" and "incredible vision" when, in God's eyes, there's no such thing as a big or small vision—there's only "obedient vision." His favor is not based on the size or scope of a vision—it's based on our obedience and fulfillment of the mission he gives us.

As Convoy of Hope continued to grow, many of us felt the weight of an expanding vision. We were now serving tens of millions of people each year: feeding children, empowering women, training farmers, responding to disasters, conducting community outreaches, resourcing churches, equipping university students, and more. The organization had graduated from pickup trucks and small garages to a fleet of tractor-trailers and warehouses around the world. The complexity of a global operation had stretched us, but team members at Convoy of Hope were diligent and hardworking. We knew God was opening doors, and we didn't want to disobey him.

One evening, despite my attempt to leave work and worries at the office, I fell asleep with a heavy heart. I was overwhelmed by a growing number of requests for aid from partners around the world. But that night, God put my mind at ease and lifted a weight off my shoulders through a dream I will never forget.

In the dream, I entered a large, empty auditorium. It was dark, ominous, and terrifying to step into the unknown. My first steps echoed against an unlit tile floor.

I asked, "Lord, are you here with me or am I alone?"

I heard no response.

"Are you here with me?" I repeated.

A deep and forceful voice filled the auditorium: "Yes—I am he."

At that moment, a spotlight illuminated a path to a side door, and I walked peacefully from the darkness into the light.

When I awoke it was 4:26 a.m. I reached for my phone to consult my YouVersion Bible app. I wanted to know where the Lord said, "I am he." The first verse I read was John 4:26, when Jesus declares to the Samaritan woman at the well, "I, the one speaking to you—I am he." (Note the time and verse are the same.) Throughout Scripture, he says, "I am he" to bring hope and encouragement to people standing at the precipice of a challenge. Undoubtedly, he was sending me a message too—to entrust all my worries and fears to him because he was with me.

Today, God is speaking to you as well. He's declaring, *I am he—the One who comforts, heals, restores, and reconciles. I know where you've been and what you're going through. Rest assured, I am he who sees all your needs and hears and answers every prayer, because what really matters to me . . . is you.*

EPILOGUE

W as it worth it?"

That was the question posed to me by a university student after I'd highlighted my thirty-year journey with Convoy of Hope.

"Absolutely!" I replied. "With Jesus, life is an amazing adventure. You don't always know where he's taking you—and often it isn't easy—but you know you are traveling with a purpose."

We did not set out to create another nonprofit organization. We began with a pledge to follow Jesus wherever he was leading. That path led us to establish Convoy of Hope in 1994. Since its inception, more than two hundred million people have been served, one million volunteers activated, and $2.5 billion in food and supplies distributed.

By 2030, Convoy of Hope anticipates feeding one million children a day, empowering two hundred and fifty thousand women and girls each year through vocational training and education, and training one hundred thousand farmers and families each year in agriculture so they can increase their yields and grow their own food. In addition, the organization will continue to work with churches and corporations to serve communities across the United States and respond to disasters around the globe.

God alone deserves the praise for what he achieves through Convoy of Hope. Jesus is our trail guide, and we are thankful to be a part of an army of compassion he is working through to transform lives and change the course of nations. And, if ever the world needed hope, it needs it now. May the love of Jesus continue to flow through you to a hurting world.

ACKNOWLEDGMENTS

Thank you to my wife, Doree, and daughters Lindsay Kay, Erin-Rae, Lauren Dae, and Haly Jay. And to my sons-in-law, Kevin and Aaron: you are a blessing to our family.

Special thanks to friends who provided insight and guidance to this project: Jan Britton, Chris Ferebee, Randy Hurst, Rich Nathan, and Brad Riley.

Thank you also to the friends who helped make this book possible: Keith Boucher, Dr. Mike Burnette, Dr. Tom Carter, Kourtney Christiansen, Dr. Aaron Cole, Court Durkalski, Roger Flessing, Brian Freeman, Dominick Garcia, Tim and Denise Harlow, Dr. Sam Huddleston, Lindsay Jacobs, Cheryl Jamison, Telvin Jeffries, Curtis Jones, Klayton Ko, Ali Lamb, Kay Logsdon, David Mayne, Tom Rankin, Sherilynn Tounger, Dr. Brad Trask, and Kirk Yamaguchi.

And to the incredible team members at Convoy of Hope: thank you for your hearts and the privilege of working alongside you.

NOTES

Introduction

1. Nicole McDermott, "Practical Types of Self-Care You Can Do Today," Forbes Health, accessed April 18, 2023, www.forbes.com/health /mind/mental-self-care/.

2. McDermott, "Practical Types of Self-Care You Can Do Today."

3. Erin Smith, "How Understanding the Brain Teaches Me to Love God Better," *Center for the Study of Human Behavior* (blog), April 20, 2021, https://blogs.calbaptist.edu/cshb/2021/04/20/how-understanding-the -brain-teaches-me-to-love-god-better/; Jeffrey M. Schwartz, "Neuroplasticity and Spiritual Formation," Biola's Center for Christian Thought, April 18, 2019, cct.biola.edu/neuroplasticity-and-spiritual-formation/.

4. Smith, "How Understanding the Brain Teaches Me to Love God Better."

5. Christina M. Pollard and Sue Booth, "Food Insecurity and Hunger in Rich Countries—It Is Time for Action against Inequality," *International Journal of Environmental Research and Public Health* 16, no. 10 (2019): 1804.

6. Steffany Gretzinger and Amanda Lindsey Cook, "Oxygen," Bethel Music, accessed August 28, 2023, bethelmusic.com/resources/blackout/oxy gen. © 2017 Bethel Music Publishing (ASCAP) / Steffany Gretzinger Publishing (ASCAP) (admin by Bethel Music Publishing). All rights reserved.

Chapter 1 Deadly Expectations

1. Ed Welch, "'I Am Disappointed in You,'" Christian Counseling & Educational Foundation, November 5, 2012, www.ccef.org/i-am-disap pointed-you/.

2. Welch, "'I Am Disappointed in You.'"

3. Michael LaBonte, "Uncle Ben Never Said His Most Iconic Line in Spider-Man's Origin," Screenrant, December 11, 2021, screenrant.com /spiderman-uncle-ben-never-said-great-power-responsibility/.

4. Nicole J. LeBlanc and Luana Marques, "How to Handle Stress at Work," *Harvard Health* (blog), April 17, 2019, www.health.harvard.edu /blog/how-to-handle-stress-at-work-2019041716436.

5. Gustav Niebuhr, "Is Satan Real? Most People Think Not," *New York Times*, May 10, 1997, https://www.nytimes.com/1997/05/10/us/is-satan -real-most-people-think-not.html; Barna Group, "Most American Christians Do Not Believe that Satan or the Holy Spirit Exist," Barna, April 13, 2009, https://www.barna.com/research/most-american-christians-do -not-believe-that-satan-or-the-holy-spirit-exist/; Pew Research Center, "Views on the Afterlife," Pew Research Center, November 23, 2021, https://www.pewresearch.org/religion/2021/11/23/views-on-the-afterlife/.

Chapter 2 Battle Scars

1. "Children's Grief Awareness Day: Facts & Stats," Highmark Caring Place, accessed April 28, 2023, www.childrensgriefawarenessday.org /cgad2/pdf/griefstatistics.pdf.

2. "For Adults Bereaved as Children," Child Bereavement UK, accessed April 28, 2023, www.childbereavementuk.org/adults-bereaved-as -children.

3. Betsy Barber, "Grieving Like God," *The Good Book Blog* (blog), October 24, 2017, www.biola.edu/blogs/good-book-blog/2017/grieving -like-god.

4. "Do Social Ties Affect Our Health?: Exploring the Biology of Relationships," National Institutes of Health News in Health, accessed April 18, 2023, newsinhealth.nih.gov/2017/02/do-social-ties-affect-our-health.

5. "Why Americans Are Lonely And What We Can Do About It," Forbes, accessed April 18, 2023, www.forbes.com/sites/sophieokolo /2023/02/24/why-americans-are-lonely-and-what-we-can-do-about-it /?sh=51c7fb7f2dbf.

Chapter 3 Reckless Ambition

1. American Psychological Association, "Stress in America 2022: Concerned for the Future, Beset by Inflation," American Psychological Association, accessed August 29, 2023, www.apa.org/news/press/releases /stress/2022/concerned-future-inflation.

2. Donald P. Coduto, *Foundation Design: Principles and Practices*, second ed. (New Jersey: Prentice Hall, 2000), 98.

3. Cambridge Academic Content Dictionary, s.v. "foothold," accessed August 29, 2023, dictionary.cambridge.org/us/dictionary/english/foot hold.

Chapter 4 The Problem with Success

1. Atlanta Magazine, "Patrick Lencioni: 'Too Many Executives Focus on the Money, Power and Pleasures' of Their Position. Here's Why It's 'Very Dangerous' for the Organization," *Atlanta Magazine*, July 11, 2021, www.atlantamagazine.com/news-culture-articles/patrick-lencioni-too -many-executives-focus-on-the-money-power-and-pleasures-of-their -position-heres-why-its-very-dangerous-for-the-organization/.

2. UNICEF Data, "Child Malnutrition," UNICEF, accessed August 29, 2023, data.unicef.org/topic/nutrition/malnutrition/.

3. Rayna Alexander, "Food Insecurity and Terrorism: What Famine Means for Somalia," Foreign Policy Research Institute, August 16, 2022, www .fpri.org/article/2022/08/food-insecurity-and-terrorism-what-famine -means-for-somalia/.

Chapter 6 Pushing Reset

1. Ashley Stahl, "Here's How Creativity Actually Improves Your Health," *Forbes*, July 25, 2018, www.forbes.com/sites/ashleystahl/201 8/07/25/heres-how-creativity-actually-improves-your-health/?sh=6f9f7 9a713a6.

2. Amanda Gabarda, "The Health Benefits of Creative Expression," UPMC My Health Matters, accessed May 8, 2023, www.upmcmyhealth matters.com/the-health-benefits-of-creative-expression/.

3. John Mark Comer, "I Am Not a Machine (Free Chapter from Garden City)," *John Mark Comer* (blog), accessed May 17, 2023, johnmark comer.com/blog/i-am-not-a-machine-free-chapter-from-garden-city.

4. "Sleep and Sleep Disorders: Sleep and Chronic Disease," Centers for Disease Control, accessed May 17, 2023, www.cdc.gov/sleep/about_sleep /chronic_disease.html. See also "Health Risks of Poor Sleep," Johns Hopkins Medicine, accessed May 17, 2023, www.hopkinsmedicine.org/health /wellness-and-prevention/health-risks-of-poor-sleep; Eric J. Olson, "Lack of Sleep: Can It Make You Sick?," Mayo Clinic, accessed May 17, 2023, www.mayoclinic.org/diseases-conditions/insomnia/expert-answers/lack -of-sleep/faq-20057757.

5. "Why Downtime Is Essential for Brain Health," Cleveland Clinic, accessed May 17, 2023, health.clevelandclinic.org/why-downtime-is -essential-for-brain-health/.

Chapter 7 Lost and Found

1. Berly McCoy, "How Your Brain Copes with Grief, and Why It Takes Time to Heal," Shots: Health News from NPR, December 20, 2021, www.npr.org/sections/health-shots/2021/12/20/1056741090/grief-loss-holiday-brain-healing.

2. Liz Szabo, "The 'Grief Pandemic' Will Torment Americans for Years," KFF Health News, June 2, 2021, kffhealthnews.org/news/article/covid-grief-pandemic-will-torment-americans-for-years/.

3. Katie Reilly, "How to Handle an Overload of Grief," *Even Better* (blog), November 13, 2022, www.vox.com/even-better/23445017/cumulative-grief-loss-overwhelming-cope-mental-health.

4. Reilly, "How to Handle an Overload of Grief."

5. Paul Tripp, "Paul Tripp's Thanksgiving Devotional: Day 11," Crossway, accessed August 31, 2023, us1.campaign-archive.com/?u=ffca6be08 f8a9a360d66dd42b&id=d6cf4899a1&e=02b14f0d82.

6. "Gratitude Is Good Medicine," UC Davis Health Medical Center, November 25, 2015, health.ucdavis.edu/medicalcenter/features/2015 -2016/11/20151125_gratitude.html.

7. Summer Allen, "The Science of Gratitude," Greater Good Science Center, white paper, May 2018, ggsc.berkeley.edu/images/uploads/GGSC -JTF_White_Paper-Gratitude-FINAL.pdf.

8. Eric Lindberg, "Practicing Gratitude Can Have Profound Health Benefits, USC Experts Say," USC News: Health, November 25, 2019, news .usc.edu/163123/gratitude-health-research-thanksgiving-usc-experts/.

9. Joshua Brown and Joel Wong, "How Gratitude Changes You and Your Brain," *Greater Good Magazine*, June 6, 2017, greatergood.berkeley .edu/article/item/how_gratitude_changes_you_and_your_brain.

Chapter 8 Yelling "Ouch"

1. Dane C. Ortlund, "Why We Need the Psalms of Lament," Crossway, May 29, 2017, https://www.crossway.org/articles/why-we-need-the-psalms-of -lament/.

2. Tim Keller, *Walking with God through Pain and Suffering* (New York: Penguin, 2013), 152.

3. The Female Quotient (@femalequotient), "It's no secret that #motherhood requires both physical and emotional strength, even if you do have the access to resources and help," Instagram, April 26, 2023, https://www.instagram.com/p/CrgnHDrMoao/.

4. "Benefits of Crying," MSU Extension: Healthy Relationships, December 4, 2018, www.canr.msu.edu/news/benefits-of-crying.

5. Leo Newhouse, "Is Crying Good for You?," *Harvard Health* (blog), March 1, 2021, www.health.harvard.edu/blog/is-crying-good-for-you -2021030122020.

Chapter 9 Next Question

1. Jill Suttie, "How to Overcome Your Brain's Fixation on Bad Things," *Greater Good Magazine*, January 13, 2020, greatergood.berkeley.edu /article/item/how_to_overcome_your_brains_fixation_on_bad_things.

2. Renee Jain, "Why It's So Easy to Be Negative (and What to Do about It)," *HuffPost The Blog* (blog), December 6, 2017, www.huffpost .com/entry/negativity-bias_b_3517365.

Chapter 10 Changing Lanes

1. Rory McDonald and Robert Bremner, "When It's Time to Pivot, What's Your Story?," *Harvard Business Review* (September–October 2020), hbr.org/2020/09/when-its-time-to-pivot-whats-your-story.

2. David Robson, "Why We're So Terrified of the Unknown," *BBC Worklife* (blog), October 26, 2021, www.bbc.com/worklife/article /20211022-why-were-so-terrified-of-the-unknown.

3. Nathan Furr and Susannah Harmon Furr, "How to Overcome Your Fear of the Unknown," *Harvard Business Review* (July–August 2022), hbr.org/2022/07/how-to-overcome-your-fear-of-the-unknown.

Hal Donaldson is the president/CEO
of Convoy of Hope, a global faith-
based nonprofit organization that
works with communities to address
root causes of poverty and hunger.
According to *Forbes*, Convoy of Hope
is among the fifty largest charities in
the United States. Through its disaster responses and community devel-
opment programs, Convoy has distributed more than $2.5
billion worth of food and supplies to more than 200 million
people, and currently feeds more than 530,000 children every
school day.

Hal has received numerous public service awards. He has
a BA in journalism from San Jose State University and a BA
in biblical studies from Bethany University. He and his wife,
Doree, have four daughters.

Connect with Hal:

 HalDonaldson.org

 @HalDonaldson

Lindsay Donaldson-Kring obtained her Juris Doctor from Washburn University School of Law. She joined Convoy of Hope's global program team in 2016 and now serves with Convoy's marketing and communications team. She is the coauthor of two books and resides with her husband, Kevin Kring, and their dog, Mel, and cat, Piper.

Convoy of Hope is a faith-based, nonprofit organization with a driving passion to feed the world through children's feeding initiatives, women's empowerment, agricultural initiatives, community outreach, and disaster response. In partnership with local churches, businesses, civic organizations, and government agencies, Convoy strategically offers help and hope to millions of people around the world each year.

Connect with Convoy of Hope:

ConvoyOfHope.org

@ConvoyOfHope

@ConvoyOfHope

@ConvoyOfHope